D0151551

Photovoltaics
and Architecture

Edited by Randall Thomas
Max Fordham and Partners

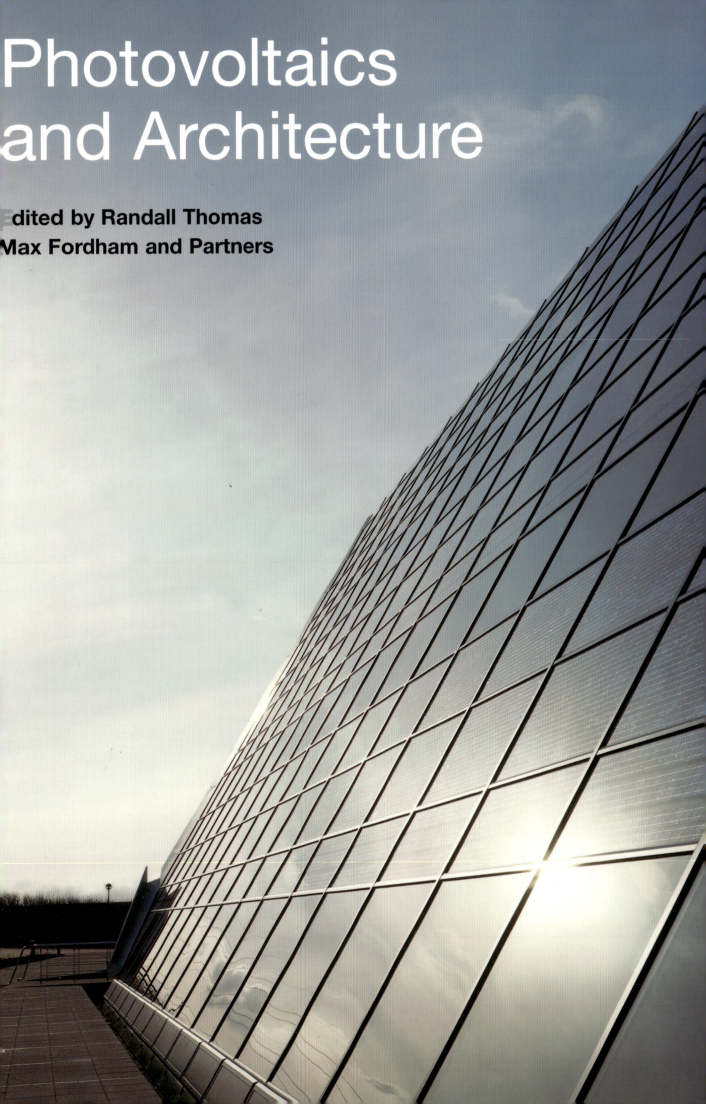

Photovoltaics and Architecture

Photovoltaics and Architecture

Edited by
Randall Thomas
Max Fordham & Partners

London and New York

First published 2001 by Spon Press
11 New Fetter Lane, London EC4P 4EE

Simultaneously published in the USA and Canada
by Spon Press
29 West 35th Street, New York, NY 10001

Spon Press is an imprint of the Taylor & Francis Group

© 2001 Selection and editorial matter: The partners of Max Fordham &
Partners; individual chapters, the contributors
Typeset in 9/11.5 Futura Light by Wearset, Boldon, Tyne & Wear
Printed and bound in Great Britain by Bell & Bain.

British Library Cataloguing in Publication Data
A catalogue record for this book is available from the British Library

Library of Congress Cataloging in Publication Data
A catalog record for the book has been requested

ISBN 0-415-23182-5

Contents

Contributors

Philip Armitage joined Max Fordham & Partners in 1988 after graduating from Durham University, and became a partner in 1992. He has worked on a wide variety of projects, including the restoration of the Savoy Theatre, London and the Royal Exchange Theatre, Manchester.

Peter Clegg is a Senior Partner with Feilden Clegg Bradley, having established the practice with Richard Feilden in 1978. Educated at Cambridge and Yale, he is a Visiting Professor at the University of Bath School of Architecture. He has more than twenty years' experience in low energy architecture, including the development of passive solar and super-insulated housing under EEC demonstration grants in the 1980s. Peter is actively involved in design, research and education at the forefront of environmental design. In 1998 he was nominated by the RIBA as Designer of the Year for the Prince Philip Awards. Peter was partner in charge on the New Environmental Building for the Building Research Establishment, and current projects include The Earth Centre, Yorkshire ArtSpace, the Yorkshire Sculpture Park, Stourhead, Painshill Park, and masterplanning a new campus for Falmouth College of Arts.

Chris Cowper qualified from Kingston School of Architecture in 1975. He worked for the GLC Department of Architecture and Design and was a member of the research group into Self-build Housing funded by the Department of the Environment. After working for Cambridge Design, he set up Chris Cowper Associates in 1980 and was joined by James Griffith in 1984. Cowper Griffith Associates is now one of the leading firms of architects in the Cambridge area.

Bill Dunster, a graduate of Edinburgh University, worked with Michael Hopkins and Partners for fifteen years before forming Bill Dunster Architects which operates from Hope House in Molesey, a prototype solar Live/work unit. He was involved with the EU-funded Joule research projects working towards zero energy urban buildings, and has taught at the Architectural Association and the University of Kingston. More recent work includes the new Michael Hopkins Jubilee campus at Nottingham University, and the mixed development urban village at Beddington in Surrey for the Peabody Trust.

Bill Gething joined Feilden Clegg Bradley in 1981, becoming a partner in 1983, and is a member of the RIBA Sustainable Futures Committee. He has special responsibility for the practice's research work and collaborated with Randall Thomas in producing *Photovoltaics in Buildings – A Design Guide*, an ETSU-funded guide for architects and engineers.

Tim Grainger studied physics and holds an M.Sc. in optoelectronics. He was with Max Fordham & Partners from 1997 to 1999, and is now doing research for his Ph.D.

Michael Keys joined Feilden Clegg Bradley in 1995, becoming a partner in 1999. He is the designer of the 1000 square metre photovoltaic installation at The Earth Centre, Yorkshire, and collaborated with Randall Thomas in producing *Photovoltaics in Buildings – A Design Guide*, an ETSU-funded guide for architects and engineers. Areas of special interest include earth building techniques and building integrated photovoltaic technology. He has taught at Portsmouth University, Oxford Brookes University and for the past three years at Bath University.

David Lloyd Jones is a director of Studio E Architects. He is a leading exponent in the design of low-energy and renewable buildings. He is also heavily involved in promotion and research in this field. Projects include the seminal NFUM&A Insurance Head Office, the photovoltaic integrated Solar Office at Sunderland and the current zero-emissions RES Head Office and Visitors' Centre. He recently published *Architecture and the Environment*.

Richard Partington worked for Nicholas Hare Architects before establishing his own practice, which specialises in urban renewal schemes and low-energy projects, in 1998. A design consultant for the Cardiff Bay Development Corporation, his work includes the prize-winning Charities Aid Foundation offices at King's Hill in Kent, the Nokia Telecommunications Research and Development Facility masterplan and the Latymer School Performing Arts Centre.

Randall Thomas is a senior partner of Max Fordham & Partners and a Visiting Professor in Architectural Science at the School of Architecture, University of Kingston. He has lectured widely on sustainable architecture in England and France. His numerous publications include *Environmental Design*, which he edited, and *Photovoltaics in Buildings – A Design Guide*, for which he was principal author.

Bill Watts MSc graduated from St Catherine's College, Oxford where he received a BA(Hons) in Zoology, and Stirling University where he received an M.Sc. He became a partner of MFP in 1982, a director in 1986, and an Engineering Group Leader in 1987. As group leader he has headed projects such as Grove Road School which won the HVAC and Independent on Sunday Green Building of the Year Award in 1993, the Avenue Estates housing refurbishment, a housing development at Milton Court Estate, a theatre and pool complex in Borehamwood and the Judge Institute of Management Studies. He was in charge of work on the warehouse at the Tate Gallery, Liverpool, the refurbishments at Chesham Place, the brief for Milton Keynes Art Gallery and an environmental study for Leighton House, a Grade II listed building, housing the work of Lord Leighton and other artists of his time. Bill is working on a number of projects using photovoltaics including Haileybury Girls' School and the offices for Renewable Energy Systems.

Foreword

Randall Thomas has done an important service to the design community by assembling this primer on basic photovoltaic (PV) concepts, practice, and field examples for the UK and northern Europe. The treatment is clear, well-organised, and practical.

Further opportunities can yield economics even better than the authors describe. Exceptionally close attention to efficient use of electricity costs far less than producing it, especially by PVs. The publications of Rocky Mountain Institute's Green Development Services (www.rmi.org) describe how highly integrated design, starting at the preconception stage, can often make highly energy-efficient buildings cost *less* to construct, due largely to making costly mechanical systems smaller or eliminating them altogether. Combined with deep daylighting and small power and lighting loads of only 2 and 3W/m^2 the annual energy demands of offices in Northern Europe can be reduced to only a few kWh/m^2. These buildings can cost several percent *less* than normal to build, have higher space efficiency, and yield superior human, environmental, market, and financial performance. As described in *Natural Capitalism* (www.natcap.org), such very large resource savings often cost less than small savings.

PVs become far more attractive in buildings that need so little electricity. PVs can also contribute to systems which provide ultra-reliable, ultra-high quality electricity such as those in the flagship New York speculative office, Four Times Square. PVs also provide constant-price electricity that valuably avoids the financial risk of price volatility and they avoid the costs and losses of the grid (generally the costliest part of the modern electricity supply system). These and scores of other "distributed benefits" can increase the economic value of PVs by roughly tenfold in most cases, making them competitive today in most applications, even in British climes. A primer on this more involved style of analysis will be published in 2001 by Rocky Mountain Institute as *Small Is Profitable: The Hidden Economic Benefits of Making Electrical Resources the Right Size*.

Many technological improvements will also make PVs ever more ubiquitous, including reversible hydrogen fuel cells that efficiently store and regenerate electricity plus valuable heat. But perhaps the most important advance will be in rearranging people's mental furniture. Buildings that are net producers of energy – and of beauty, food and water, and delight — are a key element of the better life, lived more lightly, that the 21st Century offers. I hope this book will help to launch many more designers on that path. All our lives will be the brighter for it.

Amory B Lovins, CEO (Research), Rocky Mountain Institute (www.RMI.OKA)
OLD SNOWMASS, COLORADO, 29 OCTOBER 2000

Preface

Architecture and environmental engineering continue to grow closer to each other and the use of photovoltaics in buildings is the most recent step in this development. It is not only individual buildings but also the fabric of our cities and towns which is being affected.

Photovoltaics will make an important functional contribution to sustainable development, and at least some of our buildings will become small power-stations.

In the following chapters we have provided a basic introduction to building-integrated photovoltaics (BIPVs) and case studies covering varying building types and settings. Numerous examples shown illustrate our belief that PV projects must be visually attractive as well as efficient. In many ways these are the first steps towards a solar renaissance.

We hope they will help you go further. Good Luck!

Randall Thomas

Acknowledgements

Chapters 1–6 originally formed the ETSU publication *Photovoltaics in Buildings – a Design Guide*, written by Randall Thomas (principal author), Tim Grainger, Bill Gething and Mike Keys with numerous illustrations by Tony Leitch. We would like to thank ETSU through the DTI New and Renewable Energy Program for allowing the material to be incorporated in the book and in particular Dr Julian Wilczek for his assistance. We also appreciate the ongoing co-operation and assistance of Bill Gething and Mike Keys.

We would like to thank the following people who gave generously of their time, in providing useful guidance, in showing us around PV installations, or in reviewing parts of the text of the *Design Guide*:

Mr Bill Dunster
Dr Aidan Duffy
Ms Helen Lloyd
Mr David Lloyd Jones
Dr Nicola Pearsal
Dr Susan Roaf
Ms Sara Wigglesworth

Our appreciation is also due to various manufacturers and system installers, including BP Solar, EETS (Dr Bruce Cross), Schüco (Mr John Stamp), Wind and Sun (Mr Steve Wade) and SMA for invaluable discussions and information. In addition, we would like to thank Mr Reiner Pos of REMU for his help in preparing Chapter 7; Mr Ray Noble of BP Amoco for his technical assistance in the preparation of Chapter 8; and the generous assistance given by Penoyre & Prasad and Southwark Building Design Service in the preparation of Chapter 9.

Chapters 8, 10–12 and 14 were first presented at a conference entitled "New Technology New Architecture" at Kingston University and we gratefully acknowledge their interest and support.

It goes without saying (but perhaps not without writing) that any errors or misunderstanding are due to us alone. We welcome all comments.

Note to readers

One intention of this publication is to provide an overview for those involved in building and building services design and for students of these disciplines. It is not intended to be exhaustive or definitive and it will be necessary for users of the information to exercise their own professional judgement when deciding whether or not to abide by it.

It cannot be guaranteed that any of the material in the book is appropriate to a particular use. Readers are advised to consult all current Building Regulations, British Standards or other applicable guidelines, Health and Safety codes and so forth, as well as up-to-date information on all materials and products.

PART ONE

1

Introduction

If the 19th century was the age of coal and the 20th of oil, the 21st will be the age of the sun.

Solar energy is set to play an ever-increasing role in generating the form, and affecting the appearance and construction, of buildings. The principal reason for this is that photovoltaic (PV) systems which produce electricity directly from solar radiation are becoming more widespread as their advantages become apparent and as costs fall. PVs are an advanced materials technology that will help us design buildings which are environmentally responsible, responsive and exciting. These will take a variety of forms as shown in Figures 1.1, 1.2 and 1.3. In Figure 1.1 the PVs are part of the roof structure; in the other figures they form the south-facing walls.

This book provides an overview of how PVs work and are incorporated in the design of buildings; it gives the information that designers and, in particular, architects, need. It is for those who wish to assess the feasibility of using PVs in a specific project, for those who have already decided to use PVs and want to know how to do so and for those with the foresight to want to plan their buildings for PVs in the future. The last category has its

Figure 1.1
Model of the design for a PV canopy at the Earth Centre, Doncaster (see Chapter 11)

Figure 1.2
Solar Office, Doxford (Sunderland) (see Chapter 10)

Figure 1.3
BP Solar Showcase

counterpart in designers and building owners in New York who in the latter part of the 19th century built lift shafts and fitted the lifts themselves later when finances permitted. Although most applications of building-integrated PVs are not cost-effective at present, it is anticipated that they will be in the not too distant future (Chapter 4).

We have addressed new buildings especially and covered a number of building types and sectors; much of the technology could be applied as a retrofit to existing buildings. Our focus is on PV systems which are building-integrated and grid-connected. PVs are a proven, commercially-available technology. In grid-connected systems, the PVs operate in parallel with the grid, so if the PV supply is less than demand the grid supplies the balance; when there is excess energy from the PV system it can be fed back to the grid. Building-integrated, grid-connected systems have the following advantages:

- The cost of the PV wall or roof can be offset against the cost of the building element it replaces.
- Power is generated on site and replaces electricity which would otherwise be purchased at commercial rates.
- By connecting to the grid the high cost of storage associated with stand-alone systems is avoided and security of supply is ensured.
- There is no additional requirement for land.

One of our starting points is that PVs should be considered as an integral part of the overall environmental strategy of energy-efficient building design. PVs will be a key element in furthering this approach to building and will help us move towards what we call Positive Energy Architecture, ie buildings which are net energy producers over the course of a year rather than consumers.

Another starting point was planting our feet firmly in the UK – the book deals with its weather conditions. However, as can be seen from Figure 1.4, annual irradiation is similar in much of Northern Europe (sometimes referred to poetically as "the cloudy North") and the growing PV movements in, for example, Germany and the Netherlands should encourage us.

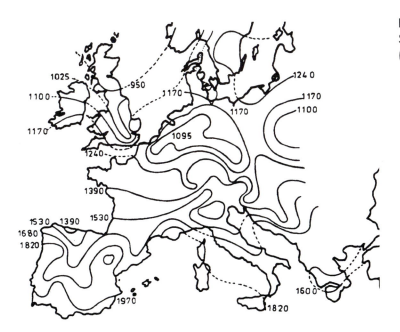

Figure 1.4
Solar irradiation over Europe
(kWh/m²/y)

The book is set out in a way that mimics the design process:

- Chapter 2 introduces some basic PV concepts.
- Chapter 3 discusses the site and building and the design options.
- Chapter 4 examines costs and sizing.
- Chapter 5 looks at the integration of PVs inside the building.

In addition we include a number of case studies, an Appendix setting out a number of technical points and a Glossary.

We have tried to set out the issues in a straightforward manner but it should be remembered that real design is always iterative, often illogical and occasionally inspired – the art is in attaining the right mixture.

We hope the book will give an idea of the variety and flexibility of PVs and of their design and aesthetic potential; if we as a design community are successful, our local and global environments will be enhanced.

2

What are photovoltaics?

Figure 2.1
Diagram of PV principle

2.1 Introduction

PV systems convert solar radiation into electricity. They are not to be confused with solar panels which use the sun's energy to heat water (or air) for water and space heating. This chapter looks at PVs and examines a number of issues of interest to designers including:

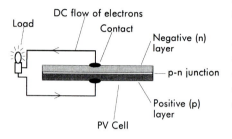

* PV module size and shape.
* Colour.
* Manufacturing technology.
* Environmental issues.
* Energy production.

2.2 PVs

Figure 2.2
Direct and diffuse radiation

The most common PV devices at present are based on silicon. When the devices are exposed to the sun, direct current (DC) flows as shown in Figure 2.1 (see Appendix A for greater detail). PVs respond to both direct and diffuse radiation (Figure 2.2) and their output increases with increasing sunshine or, more technically, irradiance (Figure A.3).

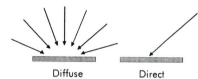

PVs are ubiquitous. They power calculators and navigation buoys, form the wings of satellites and solar planes (Figure 2.3), and are beginning to appear on cars. As we saw in Chapter 1, a number of buildings in the UK use them, eg, the Solar Office in Doxford (Figures 1.2 and 2.4).

Figure 2.3
PV modules on a solar plane

Figure 2.4
Solar Office, Doxford

Common PVs available are monocrystalline silicon, polycrystalline silicon and thin film silicon (using amorphous silicon). A typical crystalline cell might be 100 × 100mm. Cells are combined to form modules. Table 2.1 shows typical efficiencies.

Table 2.1
PV efficiencies

Type	Approximate cell efficiency[a] %	Approximate module efficiency[a] %
1. Monocrystalline silicon	13–17 (1)	12–15 (2)
2. Polycrystalline silicon	12–15 (1)	11–14 (2)
3. Thin-film silicon (using amorphous silicon)	5 (3)	4.5–4.9 (2)

a. Efficiencies are determined under standard test conditions (STC).

Theoretical maximum efficiencies for silicon are about 30%. Actual efficiencies are improving. In solar car races PVs with efficiencies of about 25% are being used. New materials such as copper indium diselenide (CIS) and cadmium telluride (CdTe) are being introduced. Novel approaches such as producing multijunction cells which use a wider part of the solar spectrum are another aspect of a drive to increase efficiency.

Figure 2.5
A Cambridge tree, near an array of 17th century solar collectors (ie windows)

It is also useful to keep efficiencies in perspective. A tree (Figure 2.5) relies on photosynthesis, a process which has been functioning in seed plants for over 100,000,000 years and only converts 0.5–1.5% of the absorbed light into chemical energy (4).

More recently, the national grid has proved only 25–30% efficient in providing us with electricity from fossil fuels.

Crystalline silicon cells consist of p-type and n-type silicon (Appendix A) and electrical contacts as shown schematically in Figure 2.6.

Figure 2.6
Crystalline silicon cell

Contact grid
Antireflection coating
n-silicon
Cell junction
p-silicon
Metal base plate
250-350 microns

Figure 2.7
Typical module constructions

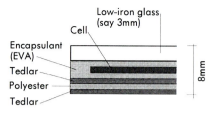

a. Glass/EVA/Tedlar™/Polyester/Tedlar™

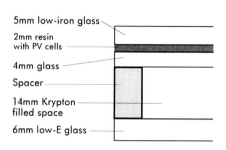

b. Glass/Resin/Glass

Figure 2.8
TFS using amorphous silicon

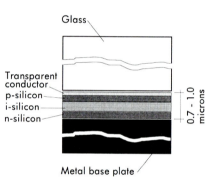

The cells, which are of low voltage, are joined in series to form a module of a higher, more useful voltage. The modules (Figure 2.7) are constructed like a sandwich (and sometimes referred to as laminates) and have a backing sheet and a cover of low-iron glass which protects the front surface of the material while maintaining a high transmissivity. A structural frame is used in a number of designs to protect the glass.

The backing sheet need not, however, be opaque. At the Doxford Solar Office (Figure 1.2), the PV cells are encapsulated between two layers of glass with transparent spacing between cells (Figure 2.7(b)); thus light passes through the transparent areas. This produces an effect inside the building which in the architect's words is like "sunlight filtered through trees".

Thin film silicon (TFS) PVs using amorphous silicon are manufactured by a vapour deposition process. Between the p and n layers is the i (for intrinsic) layer. Overall, thicknesses are much less than with crystalline technologies, hence the name. Typically, the cells are laminated into glass (Figure 2.8) but modules can also be made flexible by using plastics (Figure 2.9) or metal.

Modules electrically connected together in series (Figure A.4) are often referred to as a string and a group of connected strings as an array. An array is also a generic term for any grouping of modules connected in series and/or parallel. Power from the array (Figure 2.10) goes to a Power Conditioning Unit (PCU). PCU is a general term for the device (or devices) which converts the electrical output from the PV array into a suitable form for the building. Most commonly, the PCU has a principal component, an inverter (which converts DC to alternating current, AC) and associated control and protection equipment. PCU and inverter are sometimes loosely used interchangeably. The AC output from the PCU goes to a distribution board in the building or to the grid if supply exceeds demand.

Figure 2.9
TFS module with metal backing sheet and plastic cover

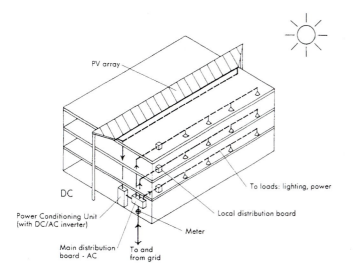

Figure 2.10
Schematic of a typical grid-connected
PV system

PV array

To loads: lighting, power

DC

Local distribution board

Power Conditioning Unit
(with DC/AC inverter)

Meter

Main distribution
board - AC

To and
from grid

Generally, grid-connected PV systems are most efficient when the array
experiences uniform conditions. This tends to favour the same orientation
and tilt for all modules, similar module and cell types and sizes, uniform
temperature conditions and so forth.

Crystalline silicon modules come in a variety of sizes and shapes, although
rectangular patterns of $0.3m^2$ to say $1.5m^2$ have been most common to
date (Figure 2.11). The weight of a 0.5m by 1.2m framed module is about
7.5kg. The laminate (without the frame) is about 4.5kg.

Larger modules of 1.5m by 2.0m have been used in installations (5) and at
least one manufacturer has modules up to 2.1m by 3.5m available to meet
the needs of the building market. With larger modules cost reductions are
possible through lower wiring costs and simpler framing arrangements.

TFS modules are commercially available up to 1–1.2m wide by 1.5–1.7m
long; the modules at the BRE (Figure 3.7(f)) were 0.93m by 1.35m. At the
smaller end of the scale, in the US, amorphous silicon is being used for
flexible PV roof shingles.

Monocrystalline silicon modules normally appear as a solid colour, ranging
from blue to black. A wider variety of colours is available but at a cost of
lower efficiency since their colour comes from reflection of some of the
incident light which would otherwise be absorbed. As an example,
magenta or gold results in a loss of efficiency of about 20%. Polycrystalline
modules are normally blue (but again other colours are available) and have
a multi-faceted appearance which has a certain "shimmer". Looking at a
polycrystalline array is a bit like looking at a very starry night sky except that
the background is blue rather than black. The appearance of TFS is uniform,
with a dark matt surface, in some ways like tinted glass; colours include
grey, brown and black. Obviously, for all PV types it is best to see several
installations to appreciate their varying aesthetics.

Figure 2.11
Module Man (with apologies to
Le Corbusier)

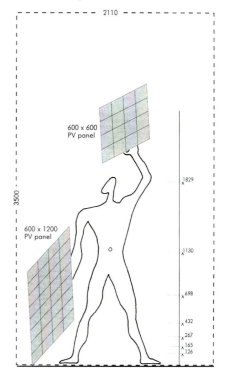

2110

600 x 600
PV panel

600 x 1200
PV panel

3500

1829

1130

698

432

267

165

126

PVs have long lifetimes. There are installations that have been in operation for 15 years or more. The design life of standard glass/EVA/Tedlar™ modules is more than 20 years; EVA is ethylene vinyl acetate. Both crystalline silicon and TFS modules are often guaranteed by manufacturers for 10 years to produce 90% of their rated output. Guarantees are designed to ensure, for example, that electrical integrity is maintained in a wide variety of varying weather conditions; the PV mechanism at the cell level itself is not the issue and will function, in principle, indefinitely. However, over long periods of time, it is possible with some types of module that water might get in, affect the junctions and thus reduce the output. Similarly, the EVA may degrade somewhat, turning yellow. Thus, we are now beginning to see guarantees worded as "at least 80% of rated minimum power for 20 years".

Environmentally, PVs have the significant advantages of producing no pollutant emissions in use and, by replacing grid-generated electricity with solar energy used mainly on site, reducing CO_2, NO_x (nitrogen oxides) and SO_x (SO_2 and SO_3) emissions.

Energy is, of course, required for their production but the energy payback period (the time for the PV installation to produce as much energy as is required for manufacture) is in the order of five years; as an example, for the monocrystalline installation at the Northumberland Building at the University of Northumbria, the figure was 6.1 years (6).

A life cycle analysis has been carried out to examine other potential environmental impacts of PVs. In general for the manufacturing processes for crystalline silicon and amorphous silicon there are no environmental issues which raise concern (7).

Some reservations have been expressed about the environmental impact of new materials, particularly cadmium telluride (CdTe). However, the production process can be designed so that cadmium is not emitted and manufacturers are actively developing recycling techniques to avoid disposal problems. The prudent approach is to keep the situation under review.

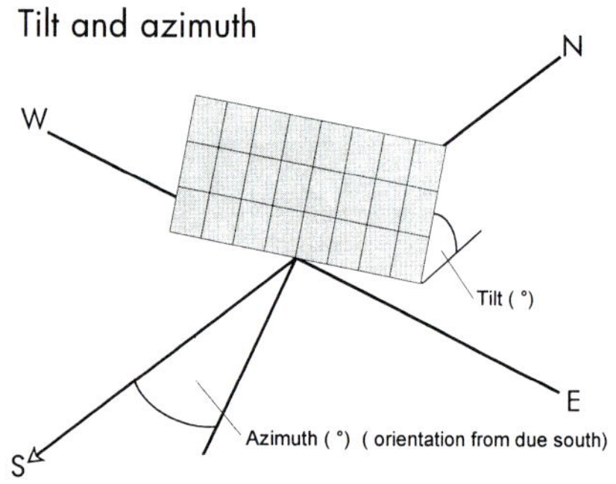

2.3   How much energy do PV systems produce?

The output from building-integrated PV installations is the output of the PV array less the losses in the rest of the system. The output from the array will depend on:

**Figure 2.12
Tilt and azimuth**

- The daily variation due to the rotation of the earth and the seasonal one (due to the orientation of the earth's axis and the movement of the earth about the sun).
- Location, ie the solar radiation available at the site.
- Tilt (Figure 2.12).
- Azimuth, ie orientation with respect to due south (Figure 2.12).
- Shadowing.
- Temperature.

For purposes of standardisation and comparison, PV modules are tested in STCs of 1000W/m² and 25°C. Thus a monocrystalline module of 1m² with an efficiency of 15% (Table 2.1) is rated at 150W peak, or 150Wp; note that this is DC (and is before conversion to AC). Arrays of PVs will often be referred to in these terms, eg the 2kWp array at the BRE Environmental Building (Figure 3.7(f)). The maximum power an installation can produce will usually be somewhat lower than the peak power. One reason for this is that 1000W/m² is a high level of solar radiation achieved only in very sunny conditions. Nonetheless, in London in clear sky conditions a south-facing wall at noon in early December can receive about 650W/m² and a south-facing surface tilted at 22.5° from the horizontal at noon in late June will receive about 945W/m². Other reasons for lower output are higher temperatures, less than optimal orientation, over-shadowing and so forth.

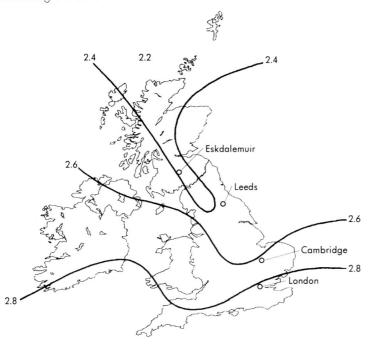

Figure 2.13
UK annual average solar radiation (kWh/m²/day)

2.3.1 Location, tilt and azimuth

While the maximum output is of value, the more important figure for grid-connected systems is the annual energy production. If we return to our list of output factors and look at location, Figure 2.13 shows a solar map of the UK and gives the maximum annual amount of energy available on a horizontal surface.

While this is useful as a guide to the basic energy available what we need to know is the total annual solar radiation on a surface tilted so that the output is maximised. This can be done laboriously from tabular data or more quickly by computer programs with meteorological data bases (computer-based design tools for PV systems are becoming more common and easier to use). Figures 2.14 to 2.17 give data for the four cities of Figure 2.13. Note that the maps show the effects of variations in irradiation as a function of orientation and tilt.

The maximum annual incident solar radiation (and hence output) is usually at an orientation of about due south and at a tilt from the horizontal equal to the latitude of the site minus 20°. Thus, Eskdalemuir at a latitude of 55°19′ N has a maximum annual irradiation of 920kWh/m²/y at an orientation 5° or so west of south and at a tilt of about 36°. An encouraging aspect is that the total annual output is 95% of maximum over a surprisingly wide range of orientations and tilts.

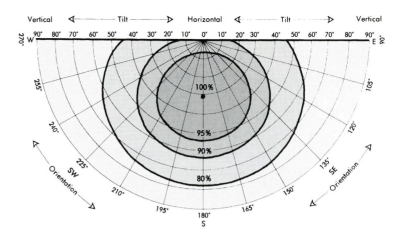

Figure 2.14
Yearly irradiation map for
London

100% corresponds to the tilt and orientation which
gives the maximum total annual solar radiation
(1045kWh/m²/y on a surface oriented due south at a tilt of 31°)
on a fixed surface in London (51°36' N, 0°03'W)

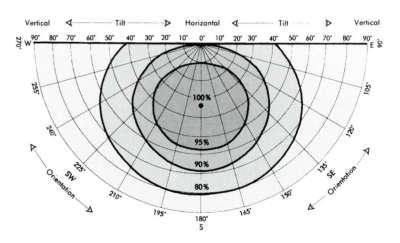

Figure 2.15
Yearly irradiation map for Cambridge

100% corresponds to the tilt and orientation which
gives the maximum total annual solar radiation
(1093kWh/m²/y on a surface oriented due south at a tilt of 32°)
on a fixed surface in Cambridge (52°13' N, 0°06'W)

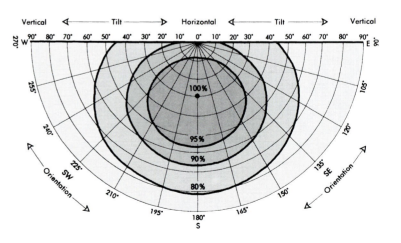

Figure 2.16
Yearly irradiation map for Leeds

100% corresponds to the tilt and orientation which
gives the maximum total annual solar radiation
(961kWh/m²/y on a surface oriented due south at a tilt of 29°)
on a fixed surface in Leeds (53°45' N, 1°30'W)

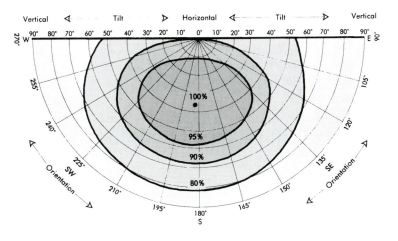

Figure 2.17
Yearly irradiation map for Eskdalemuir

100% corresponds to the tilt and orientation which
gives the maximum total annual solar radiation
(920kWh/m²/y on a surface oriented due south at a tilt of 36°)
on a fixed surface in Eskdalemuir (55°19' N, 3°12'W)

If we take a 50m² monocrystalline silicon array (efficiency 15%; nominal array power 7.5kWp) with a tilt of 20° and an azimuth of 30° (corresponding to an orientation of 150°) the uncorrected annual output, which we will call S, is:

$$50 \times 920 \times 0.15 \times 0.95 = 6555 \text{ kWh/y}$$

2.3.2 Shadowing and temperature

Shadowing will depend on the geography of the site, neighbouring buildings and self-shading by the architectural forms, all of which are considered in the next chapter; the effects of shadowing can be mitigated somewhat through system design. For the present exercise no loss due to shading is assumed.

The performance of PV modules decreases with increasing temperature (the drop in performance is more marked for crystalline silicon than amorphous silicon (Appendix A)). Designs for building-integrated PVs need to consider this from the outset in order to allow air to flow over the backs of the modules to maintain high performance. It is also likely to be necessary with all types of module to avoid unwanted heat gain into the space (which could cause discomfort and increase any cooling load). Figure 2.18 shows an approximate energy balance at a typical monocrystalline module.

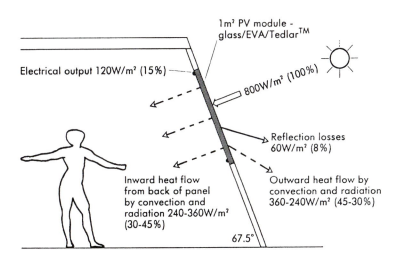

Figure 2.18
An approximate energy balance for a wall-mounted PV module (based on clear sky radiation data for London at noon on June 21). NB: All arrows are indicative only

Building-integrated modules can reach 20–40°C above ambient in conditions of high radiation (Chapter 3). For each 1°C increase in cell temperature above 25°C the power output decreases by about 0.4–0.5% (Appendix A). (So, as a very rough approximation over the year we might estimate the loss at 15°C × 0.45%/°C or 6.8%.) In practice it is easier to combine the loss due to temperature with a number of others such as dust and mismatch (Appendix A) in a correction factor we will call K, which is taken at about 0.9.

To complete the system, losses in the other components, ie the balance of system (BOS) (power conditioning unit, wiring, etc) must be accounted for, including conversion of DC to AC in the PCU. These are discussed in more detail in Appendix A – for the present a loss factor, L, of 0.8 will be used.

In summary, for unshaded installations the approximate annual energy production of the system, which we will call E, is given by

$$E = S \times K \times L$$

In the example above $E = 6555 \times 0.9 \times 0.8 = 4720$kWh/y, or approximately 94kWh/m^{2}y. A very approximate rule of thumb is that 1m^2 of monocrystalline PV array at a reasonable tilt and orientation and in an efficient system will give about 100kWh/y.

The output can also be related to the peak rating of the installation. Thus, our system with its 50m^2 monocrystalline array has an output of 4720kWh/y or 12.9kWh/day. If this is divided by the peak power of 7.5kWp we have what is known as the final yield of 1.7kWh/kWp/day; this is also sometimes seen expressed on an annual basis, in this case, approximately 620kWh/kWp. Such figures are used to compare PV systems of varying characteristics, eg size.

Another common way of assessing installations is the Performance Ratio which is discussed in Appendix A.

For comparison, Table 2.2 gives the output of a number of different 50m^2 arrays.

Table 2.2
Comparison of array outputs (MWh/y) (London data; unshaded arrays)

Position	TFS			Monocrystalline silicon		
	45° east of south	south	15° west of south	45° east of south	south	15° west of south
1. Vertical wall	2.00	2.15	2.13	3.50	3.75	3.72
2. Roof 30°	2.96	3.09	3.08	5.18	5.41	5.38
3. Roof 45°	2.86	3.03	3.01	5.00	5.30	5.26

KEY POINTS

1. PVs produce DC which in grid-connected systems is converted to AC.

2. PVs respond to direct and diffuse radiation.

3. The more sunshine, the greater the output.

4. Efficiencies range roughly from 5–15%.

5. PV cells do not let light through but modules can be constructed so that some areas are transparent and some are opaque.

6. PV systems tend to be most efficient when the array experiences uniform conditions. Designers can facilitate this.

7. Modules come in various sizes and shapes. Appearance varies with the type of PV.

8. A number of PV installations have been in operation for 15 years or more.

9. Energy payback periods for PVs are short.

10. Designers have a key influence on the following factors that affect PV output:

    - Tilt.
    - Azimuth.
    - Shadowing.
    - Temperature.

11. For grid-connected systems the annual energy production is the key figure.

12. Exact orientation is not critical. A range of orientations and tilts give 95% of the maximum output.

13. Shadowing is to be avoided wherever possible.

14. Ventilation needs to be provided to remove heat from the modules.

15. A rule of thumb is that 1m^2 of monocrystalline PV array reasonably positioned and in an efficient system will give about 100kWh/y.

REFERENCES

1.   Private communication, BP Solar, April 1998.

2.   Anon, (1996), Solar Electric – Building Homes with Solar Power. London: Greenpeace.

3.   Private communication, Intersolar, April 1998. These figures are long-term stabilised efficiencies achieved after an initial degradation of performance.

4.   Bowen, H.J.M., (1965), Introduction to Botany. Newnes, London, p. 119.

5.   IT Power, (1996), Development of Photovoltaic Cladding Systems. ETSU S/P2/00216/REP. ETSU: Harwell.

6.   Baumann, A.E., Ferguson, R.A.D. and Hill, R., (1997), External Costs of the Toledo 1MW PV Plant and the Newcastle 40kW BIPV Facade. 14th EC PVSC Conference, Barcelona.

7.   Environmental Resources Management, (1996), A Study Into Life Cycle Environmental Impacts of Photovoltaic Technologies. ETSU S/P2/00240/REP. ETSU: Harwell.

FURTHER READING

1.   Hill, R., (1998), PV Cells and Modules. Renewable Energy World, 1 (1), pp. 22–26.

2.   Anon. (undated), Photovoltaic Technologies and their Future Potential. Commission of the European Communities Directorate-General for Energy (XVII). EAB Energie – Anlagen, Berlin.

3.   Studio E Architects, (1995), Photovoltaics in Buildings – A Survey of Design Tools. ETSU S/P2/00289/REP. ETSU: Harwell.

3

PVs on buildings

3.1   Introduction

PVs offer enormous potential to building designers but, as an architect has said, "it has to be done right from the start" – they should not be an afterthought. PVs can influence the building's orientation, footprint, layout and form; they will affect the building fabric and will be an important element of the environmental and building systems. They need to be considered as an integral part of the energy strategy of the building and of its functioning. The integration of PVs with the other building elements is critical to success. Appearance and aesthetics are, as ever, especially important.

This chapter looks at the site, building type and load analysis – all factors in assessing the suitability of PVs. It then looks at the influence of PVs on the building. Because PVs are currently an expensive technology it is important to use them as optimally as possible. A parallel can perhaps be drawn with the history of glazing. In the Middle Ages, glass was expensive and each window was valued highly. Now we have them wherever we want them.

3.2   The brief

It is very important to start with a well-defined brief, ie a clear idea of what one is trying to achieve, and then to determine if PVs are applicable. If they are, they need to be part of the initial building concept and must comply with the architect's design needs as well as the engineer's functional ones.

Reasons for wanting to use PVs include:

*   Supplying on site all or, more likely, a portion of the annual electrical requirement of the building in order to reduce running costs.
*   Supplying the maximum power demand, or, more probably, some fraction of it.
*   Making a contribution to the environment.
*   Making a statement about innovative architectural and engineering design.
*   Using them as a demonstration or educational project.

The use of PVs should be part of the overall energy strategy for the building. Each project needs careful thought as the PV area required can vary enormously according to the desired goal.

PVs are worth considering if the following key factors are right:

*   Location: The solar radiation at the site is important and the building on the site needs to have good access to it.
*   Usage: The building type should have an electrical requirement that means that much of the output from the installation can be used on site.
*   Design: PVs will affect the form and aesthetics – the community, the client and the designers all need to be satisfied with the result.

3.3   Site considerations

In brief, the more solar radiation and the more uniform the radiation is on the array, the better. The location of the site is obviously of importance – generally, as one goes farther north there is less solar energy available (Figure 2.13). Edinburgh receives about 90% of the annual amount of solar energy received in London.

The topography of the site should be studied. The local wind regime should be considered as part of the strategy for ventilating the building. The matter is complex because in the winter a microclimate with low wind speeds is to be preferred as it reduces heat loss due to infiltration. In the summer, some wind is preferable as it can improve comfort during the day, assist night-time cooling, and depending on the design, improve PV performance by reducing the temperature of the PV panels (see below). The art is in achieving the right balance.

It is desirable to have a site with as little shading by hills and other geographical features as possible as this reduces the electrical output. Overshadowing by trees is to be similarly avoided wherever feasible. Because of the way PV modules are wired, shadowing from any source can have what might seem to be a disproportionate effect. This is explained in more detail in Appendix A. The implications for the architectural design are that obstructions are to be avoided wherever possible, whether they are telephone poles, chimneys, trees, other buildings or even other parts of the array itself. Where shading is unavoidable careful selection of components and configuration of the array can help minimise losses.

In urban areas overshadowing by other buildings is common. Figure 3.1 gives a very approximate estimate of losses due to shading. Computer programs are available to assist in analysing these losses

Self-shading due to the architectural form should also be avoided. Figure 3.2 indicates a few strategies to adopt.

Orientation is important but there is some flexibility for designers. It is desirable to locate the building on the site so that it is approximately within ±20° of due south; this will permit collection of about 95% or more of the energy available at a variety of tilt angles (Figure 2.14); within ±30° of due south, the figure drops slightly. The principal difference between a surface orientated 15° east of south and 15° west of south is in the period of time the radiation is received rather than its total amount.

3.4   Building type

Currently in the UK PV electricity is more expensive than that from the grid. Thus, given a building-integrated PV installation, using as much of the energy in the building makes more financial sense than exporting to the grid. The amount of PV energy usable on site is related to the size of the array and the magnitude and pattern of the demand (Chapter 4).

A wide range of building types from offices to hotels to industrial buildings can use PVs. Office blocks have good PV potential because their electricity demand is significant year-round (including the summer) and because demand is highest between 9am and 5pm. Thus, the match between demand and PV supply is good.

Houses, on the other hand, are in use in some way seven days a week but tend to use energy day and night. Nonetheless, there are likely to be individuals (and, perhaps, electricity suppliers) interested in their PV potential. Commercial and industrial buildings with large roof areas available also offer significant scope for PVs.

Figure 3.1
Shading effects by neighbouring
buildings

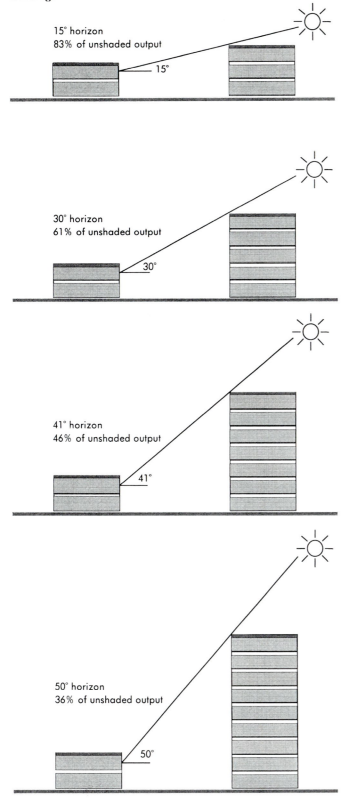

15° horizon
83% of unshaded output

15°

30° horizon
61% of unshaded output

30°

41° horizon
46% of unshaded output

41°

50° horizon
36% of unshaded output

50°

Figure 3.2
Self-shading considerations

Chimneys, ventilation
stacks etc.

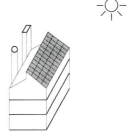

a. Put obstructions to North

Lift rooms, water
tanks etc.

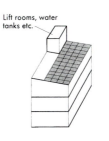

b. Put plant rooms to North

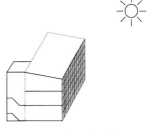

c. Ensure staircases do not shade PVs

Energy consumption, of course, varies with both type and the individual building, so a design team will need to carry out a preliminary building-specific analysis. Table 3.1 gives some indicative electrical energy demands.

Table 3.1
Annual approximate electrical energy requirement

Building	Electrical energy requirement kWh/m²/y
1. BRE Environmental Building (1)	36
2. Good Practice Office Building (non-air-conditioned; open plan) (2)	53
3. Low-energy House (3)	15–25
4. School[a]	20

a. Estimated from data in reference 4; based on 1660 hours in use per year

Figure 3.3 shows the electrical load pattern for the very energy-efficient BRE Environmental Building which was designed to improve on "best practice" by 30%. The building is not air-conditioned and the load is slightly higher in "winter" than in summer because of the need to run additional plant such as heating pumps.

Figure 3.3
Electrical energy demand of the BRE Environmental Building

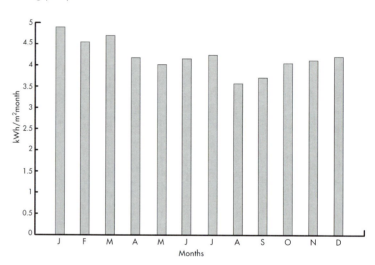

Figure 3.4(a) shows a representative annual load pattern for a house (with non-electric heating) and the output from a 1.8kWp PV installation. Figure 3.4(b) looks at a representative daily power demand pattern for a five-person household (no two households are identical) and compares it with the output from a 3kWp PV installation. Power is the product of current and

Figure 3.4
Domestic electrical demands and PV outputs

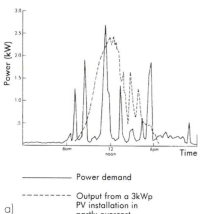

a)

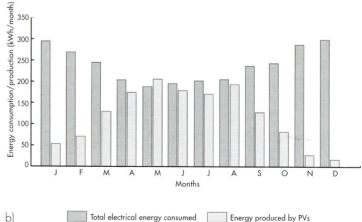

b)   ▢ Total electrical energy consumed   ▢ Energy produced by PVs

voltage and is the load at a moment in time – think of a 100W bulb, for example. Energy is the product of power and time. A 1kW load which is on for 1 hour will consume 1kWh of energy. We are all familiar with this from our domestic electricity (energy) bills.

Note the variability of the daily load (due in part to some appliances with high power requirements being used but only for short periods) and the significant evening demand when the PV output is negligible.

Figure 3.5 shows the electrical load pattern for a junior and infant school with 300 pupils compared with the predicted output from a 440m² PV array. The school has a very low installed lighting load (12W/m²). Note the much lower electricity consumption in August during school holidays.

If the site has good solar exposure and if the demand and supply pattern are reasonably matched, the design is developed further.

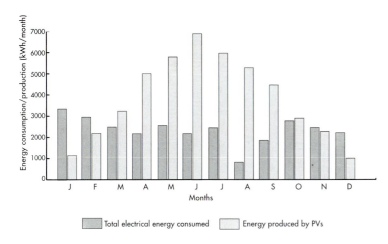

Figure 3.5
Electrical demand and PV output for a school

3.5   Design and construction

A brief guides (or effectively constrains) the design process. A certain amount of floor area will need to be located on a particular site, access to daylight will be required in many of the spaces, costs will limit floor-to-ceiling heights, and so forth. An "image" of the building usually results from the brief.

For example, a brief that made no reference to PVs but called for a typical low-energy design suitable, for example, for suburban offices, might result in the building sketched in Figure 3.6. One feature of it, and almost every other building is that it uses solar energy – for daylighting throughout the year and as passive solar gain in the winter. What PVs do is provide an additional use of the sun's energy to produce electricity.

Now, if the question, "What difference do PVs make?" were asked, what would the response be?

Firstly, in construction terms, building-integrated PV systems need to play the same role as the traditional wall and roofing cladding elements they replace. Consequently, they must address all the normal issues, for example:

- Appearance.
- Weather tightness and protection from the elements.
- Windloading.
- Lifetime of materials and risks and consequences of failure.
- Safety (construction, fire, electrical, etc.).
- Cost.

Figure 3.6
Low-energy design without PVs

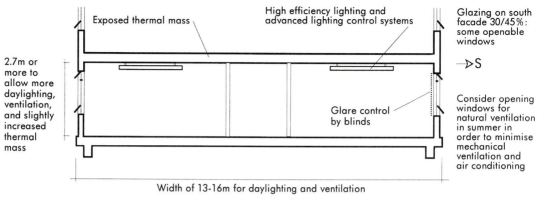

2.7m or more to allow more daylighting, ventilation, and slightly increased thermal mass

Exposed thermal mass

High efficiency lighting and advanced lighting control systems

Glazing on south facade 30/45%: some openable windows

⊳S

Glare control by blinds

Consider opening windows for natural ventilation in summer in order to minimise mechanical ventilation and air conditioning

Width of 13-16m for daylighting and ventilation

Long axis E-W to allow large south-facing elevation

In addition, there are a number of more particular aspects, often associated with being able to use the electricity produced, namely:

- Avoidance of self-shading (as mentioned above).
- Heat generation and ventilation.
- Provision of accessible routes for connectors and cables (discussed in Chapter 5).
- Maintenance (discussed in Chapter 5).

As PVs can have a marked impact on a building's appearance it is important to consult with the planning authorities at an early stage to obtain their views on the proposals.

If we look at heat generation and ventilation there are three aspects of particular interest:

1. The effect of potentially high temperatures.
2. The desirability of ventilating the back of the modules to improve efficiency.
3. The possible use of the heat from the back of the modules.

Potentially high temperatures

The potentially high temperatures associated with building elements specifically designed to capture the sun's radiation need careful consideration. The lifetime of materials, thermal movement, temperature cycling, suitability of electrical cables in high temperatures and so on need to be thought about carefully. In general, as long as the heat from PV modules does not build up and is removed by ventilation (normally, natural ventilation), there should not be a problem. As mentioned in Chapter 2, in conditions of high radiation, say 700–750W/m^2, modules can reach up to 40°C above ambient, say 70°C (5), but this will obviously depend on module design and building context. Higher temperatures can, however, occur (6) and this should be discussed with the manufacturers when considering modules.

Ventilation and modules

Chapter 2 also pointed out the importance of adequate ventilation to keep the temperatures as low as possible to improve module performance, especially for crystalline modules.

There are many ways of doing this, varying from ventilation gaps in rainscreen cladding (discussed below) to combining the module ventilation with the building ventilation (Chapter 6). A rule of thumb is to provide an air gap of 100mm (7). However, at least one study indicates that performance is improved with gaps up to 200mm or more (8).

Use of the module heat

The heat given off at the back of the panels (Figure 2.18) is potentially of value during the heating season. It is possible to use it directly or to recover it by a system of ducting – both a prototype ventilated facade (9) and a demonstration building have done this (10). However, an important question remains about the economical viability of doing so. This is particularly the case for highly energy-efficient buildings which often have very low space heating demands. (Such an office, when in operation during the day, may need no additional heat other than that from the occupants and other casual gains at external temperatures above 8°C or 9°C.) Obviously the simplest, least expensive ways of using the heat from the back of the PVs are most likely to be viable and to be adopted.

Other possibilities of using the waste heat also exist. For example, PV panels could incorporate water pipes linked to space or domestic hot water systems but such other possibilities tend to be of greater cost and complexity.

Outside the heating season, or more precisely anytime the heat is not needed, it is important that it does not cause overheating and contribute to the building's cooling load. This requires consideration of the ventilation patterns in the building and thought should be given to ensuring that in windy conditions in summer heat from the modules does not lead to discomfort.

3.6   Forms and systems

Continuing with the effect of introducing PVs into the brief, the next step might be to consider the design options.

There are three basic ways of integrating PVs in buildings:

*   Roof-based systems.
*   Facade systems.
*   Sunshades and sunscreens.

Figure 3.7 shows a number of these; non-integrated options such as PVs on independent frames on roofs and PVs on walkways and other ancillary structures are not covered here but, obviously, much of this book is also applicable to them.

The path to successful design lies between PVs imposing too great a constraint on the building and simply tacking PVs on to a form (most likely a box) that has already been designed. Real buildings have forms and angles that need to respond to more than the PV array output and this needs to be acknowledged in developing the design.

Figure 3.7
Building-integrated PVs

a) Inclined roof

b) Roof with integrated tiles

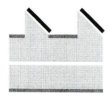

c) Saw-toothed north light roof

d) Curved roof/wall

Figure 3.7 (continued)

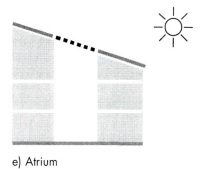

e) Atrium

f) Vertical

g) Vertical with windows

Figure 3.7 (continued)

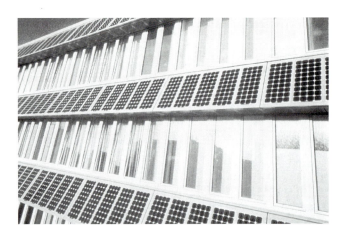

h) Inclined PVs with windows

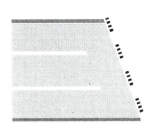

i) Inclined wall with windows

j) Fixed sunshades

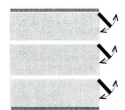

k) Moveable sunshades

Notes:
PVs are indicated by thick dark lines
Semi-transparent PVs are indicated by broken thick dark lines

3.6.1 Roof-based systems

Roofs have a number of attractions as sites for PVs:

- They are often free from over-shadowing.
- The roof slope can be selected for high performance (Figure 2.14).
- It may be easier to integrate PVs aesthetically and functionally into a roof than a wall.

Table 3.2 lists the main systems available.

Table 3.2
Roof systems

Position of PVs	System	Characteristic
1. Inclined roof	a. PV roof panels	Combined with roof structural system.
	b. PV roof tiles	Roof tiles are familiar products and are likely to find easy acceptance.
2. Saw-tooth north light roofs	a. PV panels	Allow daylighting.
3. Curved roof	a. Opaque PV flexible substrate (sheet metal or synthetic material) or rigid modules arranged on a curve	Extends design possibilities.
4. Atrium	a. PV roof panels	As for the inclined roof. Variations include part-glazing, part-opaque PVs and semi-transparent PVs.

Note that saw-toothed roofs represent a family of designs. The most common has a north-facing vertical glazed surface for daylighting. Another design in the family is transparent PV skylights set into a "flat" roof.

Ventilating roof systems

Roof systems are likely to be easier to ventilate than facade systems and any unwanted heat gains, being above the occupancy height, are likely to have less effect than for facade systems.

For inclined roof designs one approach is to have a subframe for mounting the PV modules onto the roof structure. This is shown in Figure 3.8. This allows an air space (100mm if possible) between the modules and the roof structure (which incorporates the insulation). For many saw-toothed roof designs, opening north lights can take away the heat.

Figure 3.8
Ventilated PV roof

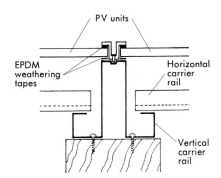

3.6.2 Facade systems

Facades have significant potential. Much PV cladding can be considered to be panes of glass to which PV cells are applied and so the extensive experience of glazed facades can be built upon. In addition, modules can be easily incorporated into other proven systems such as rain-screen cladding. Table 3.3 lists the main systems available.

Table 3.3
Facade systems

Position of PVs	System	Characteristics and comments
Vertical wall	Curtain walling	Standard, economical construction. PVs can be mixed, ie some being opaque and some semi-transparent.
Vertical wall	Rainscreen cladding	Rainscreen designs incorporate a ventilation gap which is advantageous in getting rid of heat; the gap can also be used for running cables.
Vertical wall with inclined PVs	Glazing or rainscreen cladding	PV efficiency improved. Complexity of construction increased. Potential to provide shading of windows (if desired) but a degree of self-shading.
Inclined wall	Glazing	Potentially enhanced architectural interest. PV output is improved compared with a vertical wall. Less efficient use of building floor area.
Fixed sunshades	Glazing	Can enhance architectural interest. Entails a loss of daylight.
Moveable sunshades	Glazing	Can enhance architectural interest. Entails some loss of light but less than with fixed shades. Increased PV output compared with all fixed systems.

Curtain walling systems

Curtain walling systems are a well-established technology used in numerous prestige projects such as city centre offices. The mullion/transom stick system is the most common. Vision areas are normally double-glazed and non-vision areas are either opaque glass or insulated metal panels. PV modules can be incorporated easily as factory-assembled double-glazed units. The outer pane might be laminated glass-PV-resin-glass and the inner pane, glass, with a sealed air gap between; the overall thickness of the module would typically be under 30mm.

Numerous design options are available. For example, a facade could consist of a combination of glazed areas for vision and opaque PV panels or it could have PV modules with opaque areas and transparent ones (as in Figure 1.2).

Careful consideration needs to be given to the junction box positions and cable routeing. Figure 3.9 shows a representative detail.

Figure 3.9
Curtain walling detail

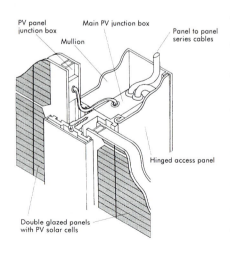

PV panel junction box
Main PV junction box
Mullion
Panel to panel series cables
Hinged access panel
Double glazed panels with PV solar cells

Note: cable containment strategy shown here is normally only used where system voltage is less than 120V.

Rainscreen cladding systems

Rainscreen cladding systems normally consist of panels (often coated aluminium) set slightly off from the building (on, for example, cladding rails) to allow for drainage and ventilation. As such they are very suitable for PV integration. The ventilation gap (which needs to be adequate, eg 100mm or more if possible for crystalline silicon (see Appendix A), and unobstructed) has the beneficial effect of reducing temperatures, thus enhancing performance; it also provides space for cable routes. Figure 3.10 shows typical arrangements.

3.7   What difference do PVs make?

Having reviewed the various systems, we can now return to the question of "What difference do PVs make to building design?"

The main points to address are:

- Orientation.
- Footprint.
- Facade.
- Section.

A building orientated to the south for daylighting, passive solar gain and free of overshading is eminently suitable for PVs. Similarly, a footprint with the long axis running east–west thus giving a large south-facing wall area and potentially a large south-facing roof is advantageous for PVs.

The facade is more complex. First, note that in many ways a wall is simply a roof rotated by about 90° and many of the issues are the same as shown in Figure 3.11. Another important point is that the solar gain through windows and rooflights is immediately beneficial (provided, of course, that it does not cause any problems, such as overheating).

The key point is that in both elements, varying requirements compete for the available surface area and thus conflicts arise. How much of a south facade should be glazed for daylighting and how much allocated to PV modules? Should a roof be all PV panels? Or none? Or something in between?

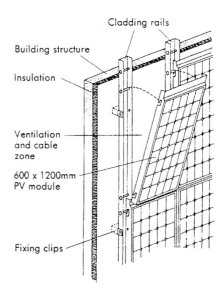

Figure 3.10
Rainscreen cladding

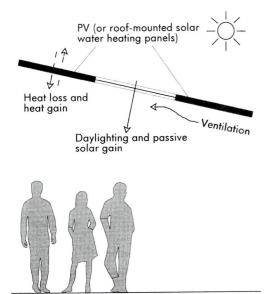

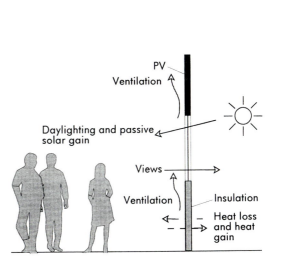

Figure 3.11
Analogy between facades and roofs

Figure 3.12 illustrates some of these considerations using a saw-tooth northlight roof as an example.

Figure 3.12
Design considerations for saw-tooth northlight roofs

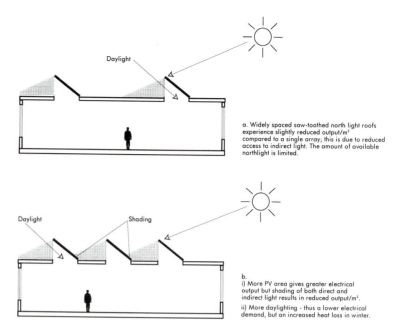

a. Widely spaced saw-toothed north light roofs experience slightly reduced output/m² compared to a single array; this is due to reduced access to indirect light. The amount of available northlight is limited.

b.
i) More PV area gives greater electrical output but shading of both direct and indirect light results in reduced output/m².
ii) More daylighting - thus a lower electrical demand, but an increased heat loss in winter.

In practice the conflicts are resolved during development of the design and the solutions are building-specific and relate back to the brief. For example, one reason a south-facing facade is unlikely to be 100% glazed is that it would probably lead to overheating (or high energy consumption for cooling) in summer. Low-energy offices, for example, have approximately 30–45% of the south facade as glazing. Thus, PVs could readily be used in much of the 55–70% of the wall that is normally opaque.

The effect on the section will depend on the size of the PV array and the system selected. Taking the easier case of the roof first, if the PVs are roof-mounted the section will tend to offset the east–west ridge to the north and perhaps vary the roof tilt angle to improve PV performance. The south facade could remain vertical or might be tilted back.

Figure 3.13 summarises the principal factors for this rather simple study. Obviously, it only touches on the issues.

Figure 3.13
The effect of PVs on the design of a low-energy office building

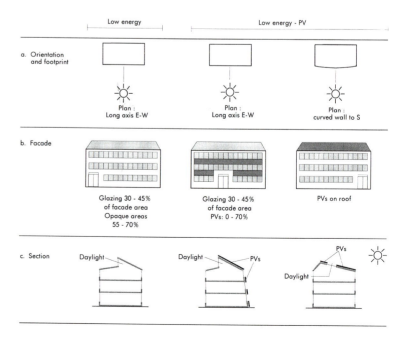

KEY POINTS

1. PVs need to be considered as an integral part of the energy strategy of a building.

2. Appearance and aesthetics are key issues.

3. PVs make a positive contribution to the environment.

4. It is essential that shading (by topographical features, other buildings, or features of the PV building itself) be minimised so as not to impair performance.

5. There should be a good match between the building's energy demand pattern and the energy available from the PV array.

6. PV modules need to be adequately ventilated so as to lower temperatures and thus maintain good performance.

7. There are a wide range of architectural ways of successfully integrating PVs with buildings and, in particular, roof and facade systems.

8. PVs can affect the orientation, the footprint, the facade and the section of buildings.

REFERENCES

1.   Anon, (1995), A Performance Specification for the Energy Efficient Office of the Future. BRECSU, BRE, Watford.

2.   Anon, (1991), BRECSU Energy Efficiency in Offices. Energy Consumption Guide 19. BRECSU, BRE, Watford.

3.   Anon, (1996), Review of Ultra-Low-Energy Homes. DoE General Information Report 39. BRECSU, BRE, Watford.

4.   Anon, (1991), Energy Audits and Surveys. AM5.CIBSE, London.

5.   IT Power, (1996), Development of Photovoltaic Cladding Systems. ETSU S/P2/002161/REP, p. 84. ETSU: Harwell.

6.   Ibid, p. 21.

7.   Sick, F. and Erge, T. (Eds), (1996), Photovoltaics in Buildings, James and James, London, p. 28.

8.   Brinkworth, B.J., Cross, B.M., Marshall, R.H and Yang, H., (1997), Thermal Regulation of Photovoltaic Cladding. Solar Energy, 61 (3), pp. 169–178.

9.   IT Power, (1996), Development of Photovoltaic Cladding Systems. ETSU S/P2/00216/REP. ETSU: Harwell.

10.   Anon, (1998), G8 Solar Showcase. Renewable Energy World 1 (1), p. 58.

FURTHER READING

Studio E Architects, (1997), Evaluation Criteria for the Review of PV-Integrated Building Projects in the UK. ETSU S/P2/00267/REP. ETSU: Harwell.

Thomas, R. (1999), Environmental Design, E&FN Spon: London.

4

Costs and sizing

4.1 Introduction

This chapter discusses the inter-related issues of costs and sizing.

4.2 Costs

In theory a PV installation can be sized and the cost calculated afterwards, much as engineers might size a heating system which is indispensable for a building. However, because PVs are an option and in the case of building-integrated, grid-connected systems, the grid supply is always available (and currently at a lower unit price), sizing and costing in practice proceed iteratively. Thus, before looking at determining the area of PV array we will examine some basic costs.

A major attraction of building-integrated PVs is that the cost of the elements they replace can be offset against the PV cost. How significant is this? Table 4.1 gives data for various conventional systems.

Table 4.1
Approximate costs of conventional systems (installed)

Wall systems	£/m²
• Cavity wall (brick exterior, block interior)	50–60 (1)
• Rainscreen overcladding (steel)	190 (2)
• Stone cladding	300 (2)
• Double glazing cladding system	350 (2)
• Granite-faced precast concrete cladding	640 (2)
• Polished stone cladding	850–1500 (3)
Roof systems	
• Roofing tiles (concrete or clay)	32 (1)
• Aluminium pitched roof	44 (1)

In comparison with these figures, Table 4.2 gives typical costs for a number of PV systems. Note that these are approximate and that lower costs can be achieved.

Table 4.2
Approximate costs of PV cladding systems a, b (installed) (4)

Wall systems	£/m²
• Rainscreen cladding systems	600
• Curtain walling using glass/glass modules	780
Roof systems	
• PV roofing tiles for a housing estate	500
• PV modules on a pitched roof of a large office	650

a. Based on crystalline silicon technology.
b. Balance of system (BOS) costs are included in the figures.

Figure 4.1
Approximate cost breakdown of a PV
installation (approximate size 40kWp)

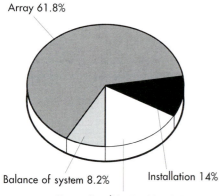

Array 45-55%

Installation 5-20% Balance of system,
Power Conditioning Unit,
wiring, switchgear,
metering etc. 30-50%

Figure 4.2
Cost breakdown of a 2kWp
installation for a single house

Array 61.8%

Balance of system 8.2%   Installation 14%

Power Conditioning Unit 16%

The breakdown of the total costs of the systems in Table 4.2 depends on the system but is roughly as shown in Figure 4.1.

Crystalline PV arrays (uninstalled) might cost between £320–480/m² (5).

The Power Conditioning Unit (PCU) is a major element of the balance of system costs. PCUs currently cost in the region of £800–1000 (uninstalled) per kW output for 3–5kW systems and less for larger systems due, in part, to economies of scale. For example, a 70kW DC to three phase AC PCU will have an uninstalled cost of about £42,000 or £600 per kW output. This works out to an uninstalled cost of roughly £70/m² of crystalline silicon module.

Metering is a small element of BOS costs. A simple one-way meter might cost £200–400 (uninstalled); two-way meters (see Chapter 5) will cost in the region of £400–700 (uninstalled).

The results of a study that looked at the cost of a one-off 2kWp grid-connected single house are shown in Figure 4.2 (6). Costs have fallen somewhat since this work was done but it remains a useful approximation. Note the higher percentage cost of the modules compared with Figure 4.1 due, most likely, to the scale of the installation. Bulk purchasing tends to significantly reduce module cost and total costs.

In general, PV systems are significantly higher in cost than conventional cladding systems. In some cases, however, such as a number of stone cladding systems of the type used in prestige office buildings, PVs could be used as cost-effective replacements.

Other cost issues, energy saved over the lifetime of the installation and cost per kWh are examined below.

4.3   Sizing the array

In sizing a grid-connected PV array there are a number of key points to keep in mind:

1.   On-site use of energy:
      For a given installation the more of the energy that can be used on site the better; this is principally because, given the current price differential between PV and grid electricity, using the energy on site makes more financial sense.
2.   Contribution to the overall load:
      Sizing is usually on the basis of a contribution to the overall load for the building rather than to meet a particular load (eg lighting).
3.   Contribution to the annual load:
      Usually sizing is to determine the contribution to the total annual load but one can also consider the contribution to the annual load during daylight hours.
4.   Available area:
      The available roof and facade area may restrict the array size, particularly in smaller installations such as houses.
5.   Budget:
      Often the available budget is the dominant constraint.

The approach outlined below is to help designers make broad decisions; actual sizing is normally done with a computer model (often a PV manufacturer's) and real weather data. Given a particular location with its solar input, a PV module type and a brief for a building, what is a sensible size of array and what will its output be? And what are the costs?

Let us examine a case where the purpose of the PV installation is to meet a reasonable percentage of the annual energy demand. In practice, one might start with a goal of, say, 20–40%; in addition, let us assume that most of the energy provided is to be used on site. Note that it is usually difficult to use 100% of the energy on site because given a varying demand and a varying supply there are likely to be times when supply exceeds demand – a simple case might be an office building with its much lower weekend demand. For our example, we will use a two-storey office building in the London area with a total floor area of 900m^2 and an extremely low electrical energy consumption of 32kWh/m^2/y. The building is oriented towards the south and is not overshadowed.

One way of proceeding is as follows:

1. Examine the pattern of the electrical demand and determine the annual electrical energy requirements of the building. In this case the base "summer" and "winter" loads were estimated to be approximately, 15 and 21kW, respectively. (The base winter load, for example, is made up of 10W/m^2 for small power, 8W/m^2 for lighting and 5W/m^2 for miscellaneous uses.) The annual electricity consumption is 28,800kWh/m^2.

2. Estimate the cost and area very approximately. From our rule of thumb, a PV installation with monocrystalline silicon panels on a south-facing tilted surface might provide 100kWh/m^2/y and the additional cost compared with conventional roofing materials at approximately £50/m^2 might be £600/m^2. Thus if the goal were to produce as much electricity as the annual demand, about 288m^2 of array would be required at an additional cost of about £173,000. The cost of a non-PV energy-efficient office building might be £800/m^2 or in this case £720,000. Thus, although the PV cost appears high we are now armed with a benchmark.

    With regard to area, the 288m^2 requirement might be fitted on the roof or on a combination of the south facade and roof.

3. Aim at some fraction of the total requirement. How one might decide what fraction is discussed below and in Chapter 6.

Figure 4.3
Unit electricity cost

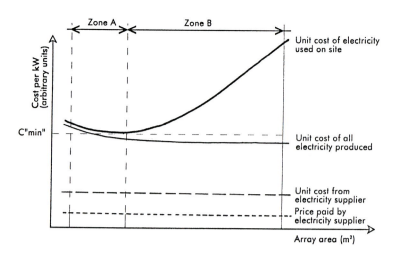

Figure 4.3 shows a graph of the notional unit cost of electricity.

The unit cost of all PV electricity produced falls with increasing array size because of economies of scale. The cost of the electricity produced and used on site initially falls (Zone A) because of economies of scale but as the array size gets larger it is likely that all the electricity cannot be used on site and so more will be exported. Since this electricity is not bought back at cost, the unit price of electricity used on site rises (Zone B).

In practice, the form of the curve and the point of "minimum" cost will depend on the specific PV installation. An approach based on sizing for the "minimum" cost, C_{min}, could be labelled the IMBY strategy, ie "in my backyard", and represents that of a client adopting a "rational" approach to their PV installation. More altruistic clients who wished to reduce CO_2 emissions for society as a whole could opt for larger arrays.

A start to a solution is to examine the load pattern. If we consider a building with a somewhat higher base power demand in winter than in summer (as is likely to be the case in naturally ventilated offices), then sizing the array to meet the summer base load will tend to ensure that the winter output (when the array output is less) will also be used on site. This is an array size which will export little energy and so is likely to be in Zone A.

If we chose to provide an array that could meet the summer base load of 15kW on a sunny day in June at noon, the sizing procedure could be:

1. Determine the solar irradiation on the array for the proposed azimuth and tilt, eg due south and 30°, giving approximately 900W/m² (7).
2. Multiply this by the efficiency of the panel, eg 0.15 and then correct for losses in the total system, eg take a factor of 0.75.

    Then the approximate power produced is:

    $$900 \times 0.15 \times 0.75 = 101W/m^2$$
    or
    $$0.10 \text{ kW/m}^2$$

3. Divide the summer base load by this figure:

    $$\frac{15kW}{0.10kW/m^2} = 150m^2$$

As before, the additional cost might be £600/m² or approximately £90,000. Again this might be considered high but it gives us another benchmark.

Note also that this part of the procedure gives a way of sizing if, for some reason, a particular load is to be met.

4. At this point, it might be decided to let a budget dominate and limit the cost of the PV installation, either as a fixed sum, eg £50,000, or as a proportion of the building cost, eg 10% of a total building cost including PVs of £800,000, or £80,000. (NB We will assume this is based on the actual PV cost of £650/m².)

    Choosing the latter, for £80,000 we would have a monocrystalline PV installation with approximately 120m² of roof panel. (Obviously, we could have a PV facade or a mixture of the two.) Since 120m² is less than that required to meet the summer base load we are in Zone A of Figure 4.3. An array of 120m² would be approximately 18kWp.

    The annual output of this system (referring to Figure 2.14) would be approximately:

    $$120m^2 \times 1045kWh/m^2/y \times 0.15 \times 0.75 = 14,000kWh/y$$

If a system lifetime of 25 years is assumed (component lifetime is discussed further in Chapter 5), the total output is 350,000kWh.

More detailed analysis would give the output used within the building, ie the on site energy savings – in this case, 75% will be assumed on the basis of results and predictions from similar buildings. This gives 10,500kWh/y or 262,500kWh over a 25 year period.

Similarly, further analysis would provide the percentage of the total annual electrical load provided by the PVs – in this case, it would be about 36%.

For a very simple measure of cost, the capital cost of £80,000 is divided by the number of kWh, 262,500, giving £0.30/kWh.

Table 4.3 summarises this and some related data.

Table 4.3
Basic data for a PV installation

• Building floor area	900m^2
• PV array area	120m^2
• PV nominal array rating	18kWp
• Installed cost of the PV system	£80000
• Total annual output of PV-generated electricity	14,000kWh/y
• PV output used within the building	10,500kWh/y
• Contribution to annual electrical demand	36%
• PV output used within the building over a 25 year lifetime	
	262,500kWh
• Simple cost	£0.30/kWh

A more detailed analysis is provided in the case study of Chapter 6.

It is also possible to do simple straight payback calculations by dividing the cost of the system by the annual savings due to supplying part of the electricity demand using PVs. The payback periods, however, are currently considerably longer than 25 years.

4.4   The future of costs

Generally, given present PV system costs and efficiencies, building-integrated PV systems are not cost-effective. Where PVs replace a range of expensive, prestige cladding, they are expected to be cost-effective after the year 2005; if supportive policies are introduced, PV-integrated buildings are expected to become commercial realities by 2010 (8). The opinion of the industry is that building-integrated PV systems will achieve wider economic viability between 2010 and 2020 (9).

Costs have fallen significantly over the past 10–15 years and are expected to continue to do so. The driving forces for this include:

1.   Increased module efficiencies. For example, efficiencies of crystalline silicon modules are expected to increase by one quarter between now and 2010 (10).
2.   Development of lower-cost thin film and other technologies.
3.   Lower production costs as a volume market leads to, for example, improved manufacturing techniques and starts to drive costs down.
4.   Reduced system costs. For example, the costs of components such as PCUs are expected to fall.
5.   Reduced installation costs as the market develops and experience is gained.

In the meantime, PVs in buildings provide direct environmental advantages and also serve as a statement of environmental interest.

An important environmental benefit is a reduction in CO_2 emissions. In the example above, which can be taken as representative, each square metre of PV panel will avoid approximately 1800kg of CO_2 emissions over a 25 year lifetime. (This includes the CO_2 emissions avoided by exported energy.) At present, it is difficult to add CO_2 emissions and money, but that situation could change.

KEY POINTS

1. The cost of PVs can be offset against the cost of the building elements they replace. Nonetheless, PV costs are presently high.

2. Sizing a PV installation tends to be an iterative process in which energy requirements, area available and costs are examined.

3. PV electricity replaces conventionally-generated power and so provides an environmental benefit of reduced CO_2 emissions. At present this is difficult to evaluate monetarily.

REFERENCES

1. Davis, Langdon and Everest (Ed.), (1998), Spon's Architects' and Builders' Price Book. E&FN Spon: London.

2. ECOTEC, ECD and NPAC, (1998), The Value of Electricity Generated from Photovoltaic Power Systems in Buildings. ETSU S/P2/00279/REP. ETSU: Harwell.

3. Ibid., p. 23.

4. Ibid., p. 23.

5. Ibid., p. Case 2a.wk4.

6   Greenpeace with original research by Halcrow Gilbert Associates, (1996), Building Homes with Solar Power. Greenpeace, London.

7   Solar Radiation data is available from a number of sources including the CIBSE Guide.

8. See reference 2, p. 84.

9. See reference 2, p. 52.

10. See reference 2, p. 24.

PVs in buildings

5.1 Introduction

Having determined that PVs are suitable, and having done an approximate load analysis and sizing of the array, the designer can move on to selecting the components and developing their integration within the building. This chapter examines a number of these aspects of the PV system.

5.2 Grid-connection and metering

Figure 5.1 shows a grid-connected PV installation, thus developing Figure 2.10 in more detail. Obviously, it is notional – the actual design will require the services of electrical engineers. Note that the inclusion and arrangement of components will also vary with the system and the manufacturers.

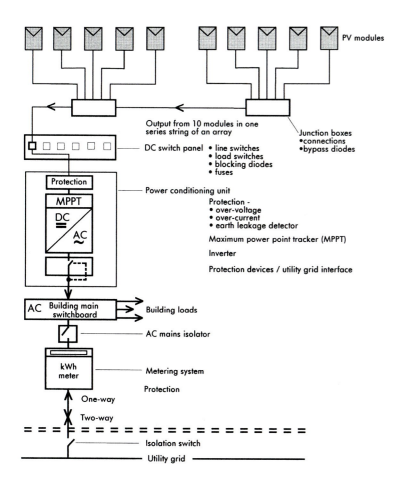

PV modules

Output from 10 modules in one series string of an array

Junction boxes
•connections
•bypass diodes

DC switch panel • line switches
• load switches
• blocking diodes
• fuses

Protection

Power conditioning unit

MPPT

Protection -
• over-voltage
• over-current
• earth leakage detector

DC
AC

Maximum power point tracker (MPPT)

Inverter

Protection devices / utility grid interface

AC Building main switchboard

Building loads

AC mains isolator

kWh meter

Metering system

Protection

One-way

Two-way

Isolation switch

Utility grid

Figure 5.1
A grid-connected PV installation

Starting with the grid, it is essential to contact the electricity supplier early on and obtain its permission to connect, whether or not any electricity will be exported to the grid (and similarly whether or not it will be paid for). Clients with grid-connected PV buildings will need to ensure that the installation will cause no safety hazards and will comply with technical regulations and recommendations, and that the quality of the power will be acceptable for export to the grid. For example, the grid's electricity suppliers are likely to require that, in the event of a loss of mains power, the PV installation will close down automatically. This is to give the grid maintenance engineers a dead system on which to carry out repairs. As one supplier says, their guideline to customers is that "you must not interfere with anyone else".

It is also important to check early on whether the supply authority will pay for any electricity exported as this has an impact on the economics of the system (as mentioned in Chapter 4). The answer may vary from not paying at all to payment of some part of the cost of producing the electricity. Whether there will be any significant additional charges for operating an embedded generator (ie a private generator connected to the grid) should also be checked.

Metering grid-connected systems is an area currently in flux as the opening up of the electricity market leads to changes to supply and metering arrangements. Leaving aside the more technical considerations, the basic options are:

1. One-way metering:
    Metering on the incoming supply and no metering on the PV output.
2. Two-way metering with two meters:
    One meter for energy imported from the grid and one for energy exported to it.
3. One meter run two ways:
    In a number of countries outside the UK where the buying and selling prices are the same, one meter is used and run backwards when energy is exported to the grid.

The metering strategy to adopt will follow from discussions with the supplier. Metering is a changing field – future developments will include electronic meters and, in 2000, the right for customers to buy meters in an open market.

5.3   System considerations

The building main switchboard in a typical domestic installation is single phase 230V AC and, in larger buildings, three phase 415V AC. Thus, the DC output of the PV arrays (Figure 5.1) needs to be converted to AC. PV modules are often at very approximately 12V or 24V (this may in fact be 18.5V at maximum power for a typical monocrystalline module). The modules are normally connected in such a way as to produce a higher voltage from the array (Figure A.4) with the exact voltage depending on the system. In electrical systems, up to 120V DC is defined as extra low voltage and from 120V to 1500V (between conductors) DC is low voltage. A broad range of voltages from, say, 50V to over 700V is in use in building-integrated PV applications. At the BRE Environmental Building (Figure 5.2) the output from the 2kWp array is a nominal 96V DC. At the Doxford Solar Office (see Chapter 10), the output from the 74kWp array is a nominal 350V DC. The choice of voltage is determined by a number of conflicting factors. Higher voltages are favoured because of lower power losses but lower voltages tend to be safer. Array configuration, PCU selection and cable selection are also important considerations.

Figure 5.2
PV installation at the BRE
Environmental Building

a) Array (left)
b) Power conditioning units
(below, left)

Figure 5.3
Alternative inverter arrangements

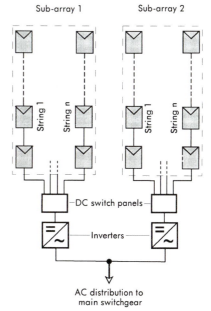

a) Sub-array inverters

Power Conditioning Units

The PCU shown in Figure 5.1 is integral to the optimal and safe operation of the PV installation. In grid-connected systems it is likely to contain:

- An inverter for DC to AC conversion.
- A maximum power point tracker (Appendix A) which may be part of the inverter.
- Protection devices on the DC side.
- Protection devices on the AC side/utility interface.

The inverter converts the DC output of the array to an AC which is compatible with the grid's voltage, phase, power factor and frequency characteristics. Inverters can operate over a range of voltages – for example, at the BRE Environmental Building the inverter is set at a voltage range of 75–150V DC and converts to 240V 50Hz AC.

Figure 5.1 is a typical single inverter configuration – other options are shown schematically in Figure 5.3. The choice depends on a number of factors including the module configuration, accessibility, cost, over-shadowing, and plant room planning.

In Figure 5.3(a) the array has been divided into two halves, or sub-arrays, each supplying one inverter. This can be a way of reducing DC cabling losses but needs to be balanced against the cost of two inverters rather than one.

In Figure 5.3(b) string inverters are shown. These can similarly help reduce the amount of DC wiring required for larger installations and also lead to lower voltages.

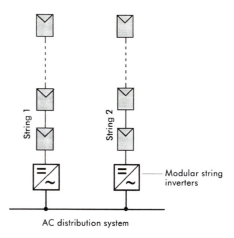

b) String inverters

Correct inverter selection is essential because the electrical output of the system depends greatly on its performance. Given the high capital cost of PV systems it is important to optimise the value of all components including the inverter.

In the UK the installation will usually be operating at well below the nominal array power. An approximate estimate is that the average output during daylight hours might be only 15–20% of the nominal array rating. Normally an inverter will be selected on the basis of the following:

- Rated power: The inverter rating is normally 75–80% of the array rating. This is discussed in Appendix A.
- Efficiencies: Modern inverters can achieve efficiencies of over 90%.
- Self-consumption losses: A small amount (say 0.5–4%) of the rated DC power is needed for the inverter to operate.

Inverters may also incorporate the utility grid interface and provide an automatic disconnect feature if the grid supply is lost and automatic restart after the grid fault is cleared.

Although inverters are electronic solid state devices and have no moving parts they can produce a humming noise. This and their need for ventilation are discussed below.

PV systems (as other electrical systems) have some significant advantages over water-based solar heating systems in that they are easier to design, install, operate and maintain. In addition, compared to other electrical systems, PVs with their lack of moving parts and high reliability of components require little maintenance. Maintenance of the array exterior simply consists of cleaning the glass to remove grime and dust occasionally as part of a normal building maintenance program.

As with other electrical systems, PVs should be examined regularly to check against any damage to equipment or cables, loose connections, and so forth. The PCU should be checked from time to time in accordance with the manufacturers' instructions. PCUs are normally guaranteed for one or two years and have an expected lifetime of 20 years or more.

PV modules and PCUs specified should meet the relevant international standards.

Safety

The integration of PVs with the building should be considered in terms of construction and access for maintenance, in the normal way following the CDM (Construction Design and Management) Regulations.

Safety is a standard consideration with all electrical installations. Contact with the front surfaces of the modules poses no danger. The particular issues that apply to PVs are:

1. Current is produced during a wide variety of light conditions and so to "switch off" the installation one needs, for example, to cover the modules with something opaque.
2. There is less familiarity within the building industry with DC compared with AC.
3. Voltages can be higher than the familiar 240V single phase AC.

Safety issues should be well documented for both installers and maintenance personnel.

Earthing and Lightning Protection

The basic issues are set out briefly in Appendix A.

Monitoring

Monitoring of the installation is useful because, as a minimum, it allows identification of any problems in operation and helps the performance of the system to be reviewed. More extensive monitoring will provide additional information such as a detailed comparison of actual output with initial predicted figures.

5.4   Modules and cables

Normally PV modules have junction boxes at the rear which contain space for connections and may contain bypass diodes (see Glossary). The modules are normally linked by "daisy chains" (ie cables loop in to one module and then out to another) as shown in Figure 5.4, a photograph of an independent roof-mounted PV installation in Dublin.

Figure 5.4
Junction boxes on a free-standing roof-mounted installation

Figure 5.5 shows another grouping of junction boxes and a drawing of a similar type of box.

Figure 5.5
Junction boxes

a) Junction boxes

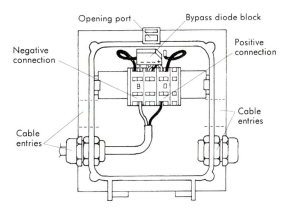

b) Module junction box

Cables join the PV components together and as for any electrical installation they need to be suitable for their environment and for the loads carried. Thus, where cables are run in areas subject to heat build-up at the rear of modules, their size will need to be increased to allow for the higher temperatures. Similarly, if cables are run where water vapour can enter, eg in rain screen cladding systems, the cables, cable ways and junction boxes must be suitably selected.

Cables should generally be inaccessible to occupants but accessible to maintenance personnel. Figure 5.6 is a view from the interior of the back of the facade at the Doxford Solar Office (see Chapter 10) where the cables are run neatly and safely in the mullions and transoms.

Figure 5.6
Cable ways at the Doxford Solar Office

Cables are usually double insulated and may be single core or multi-core. A technical issue worth mentioning here is that, with PVs, protection against certain potential conditions such as faults to earth need to be dealt with at the design and installation stage – specialists will advise on the measures (which are likely to include double insulation) to be taken.

Routes should be as short as practical to facilitate installation and to minimise cost and voltage drop. A rule of thumb is to limit the voltage drop from array to PCU to 2.5% or less. An example of cable size is given in Chapter 6.

The numerous cables involved obviously need to be considered carefully to avoid marring the building's aesthetics. This is a particularly important issue with PV cladding systems and also where arrays are semi-transparent.

Future developments

The DC systems most commonly in use (which are the basis of this chapter) have the disadvantages of being less familiar than AC, of requiring more specialised equipment and of sometimes operating at higher voltages. Consequently, work is being carried out to integrate the PV module with the inverter to produce AC-modules. These could lead to lower design and installation costs and facilitate the acceptability of PV. Such systems are available but have not yet been widely used in the UK.

5.5   Plant rooms

Ideally the plant room will be as close to the PV array as possible for ease of routeing and to minimise energy losses in the cables.

In a domestic installation of say 3kWp the PCU might be wall mounted inside a closet along with the incoming mains supply and meter. The PCU might take up a space 600mm high by 400mm wide by 150mm deep.

In larger buildings the plant room is likely to have the following:

*   The DC switchgear.
*   The PCU.
*   The main AC switchgear.
*   The mains incomer and meters.

If the PV installation is monitored as is recommended, space should also be allocated for the equipment.

The space requirement for the DC switchgear and the PCU is obviously additional to that of the normal electrical plant room and will vary with the size of the installation. At the 2kWp BRE Environmental Building the DC switches and PCUs are wall mounted (Figure 5.2) and the additional space requirement is no more than, say, 1.5m^2 of floor space. At the 39.5kWp Northumberland Building (Figure 3.7(h)) the approximate dimensions of the DC switch panel and the PCU are 2.0m W × 2.0m H × 0.4m D and 2m W × 2m H × 0.6m D, respectively. The floor area used is about 12.5m^2 (but perhaps could be reduced slightly). A very rough rule of thumb is an additional plant room area equal to 3–5% of the array area is required if a single PCU or several large sub-array PCUs are used.

The small PCUs at the BRE are quiet but larger units can produce a significant "hum" as mentioned above. One guideline for specifiers suggests a limitation of 55dBA for PCUs (a modern, "quiet" dishwasher produces about 45–50dBA).

Switchgear is robust and will function adequately at temperatures from −4°C to 40°C; it must of course be protected from the weather. The manufacturers' requirements should be checked for both switchgear and PCUs. A typical large PCU might require a temperature range of 1°C to 38°C. As much as 5–10% of a PCU's nominal output can be lost as waste heat and so ventilation will be required to prevent excessive temperatures. Normally, supplementary heating will not be needed but, as this depends on the building construction, the ventilation system etc needs to be checked for each building.

Access to the plant room should be restricted as is common practice.

KEY POINTS

1. Grid-connected PV installations convert DC from the PV arrays into AC for use in the building with any unused power being exported to the grid.

2. There are a number of alternative array configurations and inverter arrangements. The selection will depend on factors such as module configuration, accessibility, cost, overshadowing and plant room planning.

3. PCUs have an expected lifetime of 20 years or more.

4. Safety is, as ever, a paramount consideration. The particular issues of PV electricity such as the production of current in a wide variety of light conditions need to be known to all.

5. Monitoring of the installation is useful for identifying any problems and for reviewing performance.

6. PV cable runs need to be integrated with the building design.

7. Plant room space needs to be allotted for the PCU and associated equipment. The plant room needs to be ventilated.

FURTHER READING

1. Halcrow Gilbert Associates, (1993), Grid Connection of Photovoltaic Systems. ETSU S 1394-P1, ETSU: Harwell.

2. Halcrow Gilbert Associates, (1993), Guidelines on the Grid Connection of Photovoltaic Systems. ETSU S 1394-P2, ETSU: Harwell.

3. Munro, D. and Thornycroft, J., (Undated), Grid Connecting PV Buildings. In 21 AD Architectural Digest for the 21st Century Photovoltaics, Eds. Roaf, S and Walker, V. Oxford Brookes University.

4. Sacks, T., (1997), Shadows Loom Over the Solar Era. Electrical Review 27 May – 4 June, pp. 25–28.

5. Newcastle Photovoltaics Applications Centre. Architecturally Integrated Grid-Connected PV Facade at the University of Northumbria. ETSU S/P2/00171/REP, ETSU: Harwell.

PART TWO

6

Cambridge Botanic Garden, Cambridge, UK

Randall Thomas

6.1   Introduction

This chapter discusses the preliminary design of a building-integrated PV system. It is broadly based on a new-build project for the Cambridge Botanic Garden but has been simplified and developed (1). The intention is to provide a visitors centre/office accommodation and a bowls club under a single roof. This rather unusual combination of facilities is due in large part to the presence of an existing bowls club on part of the site which is to be demolished to make room for the new facilities.

6.2   Site and brief

Cambridge enjoys a moderate amount of sunlight (981kWh/m²/y on a horizontal surface), is temperate (mean annual temperature 9.6°C; mean temperature June to August 15.7°C), and is fairly dry (mean annual rainfall 540mm).

Figure 6.1 shows the site plan.

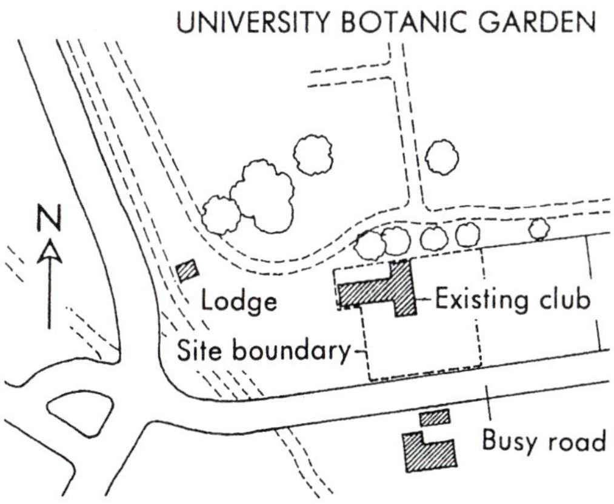

The flat site (typical of much of Cambridgeshire) is bordered on the north by the Botanic Garden and on the south by a busy road.

The brief called for:

- A total gross area of about 3950m² divided into:
    a. an exhibition and information/teaching area of 650m²
    b. administrative offices of 1300m²
    c. a six-lane indoor bowling green with associated changing rooms and WCs; area about 1600m²
    d. a cafe/bar of 400m².
- An external bowling green.
- Car parking facilities.
- Reasonable capital costs – as yet not defined at this early stage.

The client has a professional, special interest in environmental design and instructed the design team to develop an integrated, low-energy approach and examine energy, materials, water use and waste recycling in detail. Under the energy topic three particular areas were identified for investigation:

- The use of PVs.
- Daylighting of the indoor bowling green (to reduce the artificial lighting energy demand).
- Natural ventilation of all spaces.

Preliminary site analysis led to the initial concept shown in Figure 6.2.

This was principally to link the visitors centre and offices to the Botanic Garden as well as to distance them from the noise and pollution of the road. The footprints of the bowling greens are defined by functional requirements; the visitors centre and offices are more flexible.

Figure 6.1
Site plan

UNIVERSITY BOTANIC GARDEN

Lodge
Site boundary
Existing club
Busy road

Figure 6.2
Initial site planning

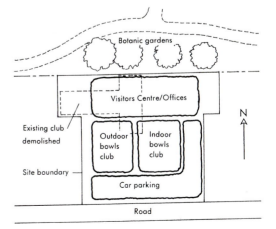

Botanic gardens

Visitors Centre/Offices

Existing club demolished

Outdoor bowls club

Indoor bowls club

Site boundary

Car parking

Road

Figure 6.3
Building massing

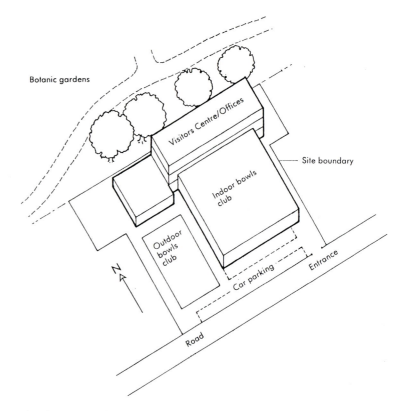

The design team then began to examine what the implications on form would be with particular attention to PVs and daylighting. The team knew that PVs were not normally immediately financially viable but needed to set out the facts to the client and wished, as far as possible, to allow for future flexibility.

From the brief it was possible to develop the design. As daylighting of the bowling green (particularly) needed to be fairly uniform, this part of the building was likely to be single storey, say, about 5.5m in height. Building costs favoured a two or three storey visitors centre and offices area; however, this would make the building more prominent from inside the Garden. After considerable discussion with all concerned parties, including the planners, a three storey proposal was adopted. The massing shown in Figure 6.3 resulted. Internal planning was also considered and, particularly, the area to the north of the wall separating the bowling green and visitors centre. It was thought that this zone would be used for spaces without a daylighting requirement such as WCs or with a need for blackout such as conference rooms.

The design team continued their initial assessment of PV feasibility by looking at a number of factors including:

*   Suitability of the site in general.
*   Availability of surface area.
*   Occupancy of the building and load.
*   Likely array size, cost and generation pattern.

Simultaneously, to avoid abortive work, preliminary discussions took place with local planners and the electricity supplier in order to assess whether PV proposals were likely to be considered favourably. The response was encouraging in both cases.

Site

The site is free of obstructions and was judged to be very suitable. There is some potential loss of north sky diffuse radiation due to the Garden's tall trees but this is not significant. Since the buildings face south and the car park and road are "dead" zones, there is very good solar access.

Surface area

To assess this required further development of the building form. Based on common practice in low-energy office design (Chapter 3) it was decided that the visitors centre/office should aim at a floor width of about 15m at most to allow for natural ventilation. Thus, the form of the visitors centre/office area was confirmed as a rectangular block with the long axis running east–west.

As for the indoor bowling green, it was necessary to study the daylighting in more detail to determine the area left for PVs on either the roof or south wall. Discussion with indoor bowlers (who sometimes have a marked aversion to daylight) convinced the design team that direct sunlight needed to be excluded and that good uniformity of daylight over all lanes would be required. Thus, a roof lighting scheme was selected. For architectural interest, to avoid the factory-like appearance of normal saw-tooth northlight roofs and potentially to increase the PV capacity a concept sketch of successive "waves" was drawn (Figure 6.4).

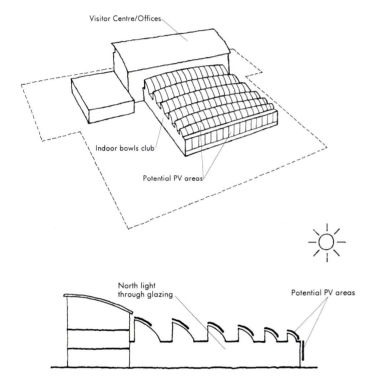

Figure 6.4
Roof proposal

The daylight factor of 6–8% required to provide 500 lux for bowling much of the time without artificial lighting meant that the bowling green roof area available for PVs was about 750m². In addition the upper portion of the south facade (leaving the lower part free because of shading by cars) with an area of 60m² was available and the roof of the offices with a plan area of 650m² was potentially available. The module loads were assessed structurally and it was considered that they could easily be accommodated.

Occupancy and load

The likely occupancy of the building is favourable to PVs as indoor bowling takes place from 9am until 9pm seven days a week throughout the year. The visitors centre will also be in operation seven days a week throughout the year; the offices will be occupied on weekdays. Overall, this means that there will always be a load on site for the PVs to supply and therefore less electricity will be exported.

The loading of the building had to be examined in detail. For the visitors centre and office area an electrical consumption of 30–35kWh/m²/y was estimated based on an energy-efficient building (Chapter 3). For the bowling green each aspect (artificial lighting, small power for cafe/bar, etc.) was studied resulting in an estimate of 35–40kWh/m²y. Figure 6.5 shows the annual energy demand pattern (and PV supply – see below); Figure 6.6 shows a typical weekly power demand in summer.

Figure 6.5
Annual electrical demand and PV supply

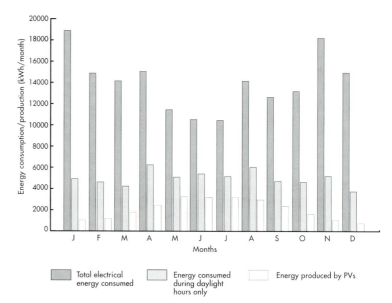

Figure 6.6
Weekly demand pattern

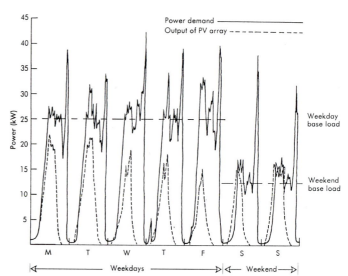

Array size and cost

As can be seen from Figure 6.6 the typical summer daytime minimum power demand or base load is 25kW during the week and 12kW at weekends; during the winter it is slightly higher because of additional lighting and plant loads, eg heating pumps.

If the PV installation were sized to provide an on-site maximum of 25kW in summer we would be fairly confident of being able to use most of the energy produced on site (because supply will usually be less than the base demand).

At this stage assuming a performance ratio of 0.75 (to account for system losses) leads to a nominal required array rating of about 33kWp to meet the summer base load. The output from this array for a typical week in June is also plotted in Figure 6.6.

If monocrystalline silicon cells were used this might require an area of approximately 235m² and might entail an installed cost of about £150,000 (Chapter 4).

At this point the design team knew the area required was available but did not know if the client had the money. In the meantime, the approximate cost of the building was estimated at £900/m² or £3,550,000 without PVs, so the PV cost would represent very roughly (allowing for partial replacement of the metal roofing system that had been costed) about 5% of the building cost.

The design team then met the client to present its findings. There was some disappointment at the cost and the fact that the entire roof would not be PV modules. There was discussion about whether the electricity supplier would pay for energy exported and, if so, how much. As the answers were not known, it was decided to err on the side of caution and discount any contribution for the time being. In the end, the additional cost was judged to be acceptable and worthwhile on the basis of the percentage of the building cost, the environmental benefits and the educational value.

In order to make the maximum public statement about the installation, the client requested that the PV modules be at the southernmost part of the bowling green roof and on its south facade. He also asked that the remaining bowling green roof be designed so that it could be used for PVs in the future when costs had fallen. The design team returned to their drawing boards (or more precisely their computer screens).

6.3   Design development

The following aspects of the design were then developed:

*   Optimisation of the daylighting and PV capability of the roof.
*   PVs and the natural ventilation strategy.
*   Choice of module.
*   Sizing and costing.
*   System considerations.
*   The PV installation inside the building.

Daylighting and PVs

The initial assumption of a daylight factor of 6–8% was maintained and a uniformity ratio of about 0.5 specified. Numerous configurations were studied using computer modelling – Figure 6.7 shows three of them.

The main conclusions of the exercise (which looked at electrical energy but did not go into energy for space heating which was thought to be a lesser consideration) were:

*   The optimum angle for a stand-alone array in Cambridge is about 31°; this is consistent with the rule-of-thumb of latitude less 20°. A uniform roof based on this has a comparatively low daylight factor, thus higher electrical costs.
*   By increasing the angle to 45° daylight is improved; the PV output, however, drops because the angle is not optimal and self-shading losses are higher.
*   If the 45° tilt is maintained, increasing the height of successive ridges reduces self-shading and increases the PV output. The daylight factor, however, drops slightly.

Figure 6.7(c) suited the initial "wave" concept, provided good daylighting and offered significant PV potential. There was a great deal of discussion about the increased structural complexity and costs resulting from non-uniformity and the appearance of the roof from the inside but, in the end, it was agreed to take forward this design.

Figure 6.7
Roof configurations

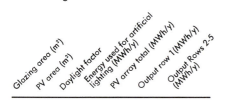

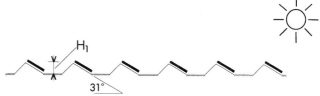

a. Uniform height (H₁), each south face 100% PV, each north face is 100% glazing; PV tilt 31°

Glazing area (m²)	PV area (m²)	Daylight factor	Energy used for artificial lighting (MWh/y)	PV array total (MWh/y)	Output row 1 (MWh/y)	Output Rows 2-5 (MWh/y)
510	696	6.1	56	101.5	17.6	16.8
684	684	8.0	42	94	16.8	15.4
684	684	7.8	43	95.2	16.8	15.7

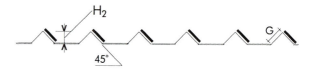

b. Uniform height (H₂), each south face 100% PV, each north face is 100% glazing; PV tilt 45°

c. Increasing height, front (smallest) tooth identical to any tooth in b, subsequent teeth have equal areas of PV and glazing to front tooth; PV tilt 45°

Figure 6.8
Services strategy and notional air paths

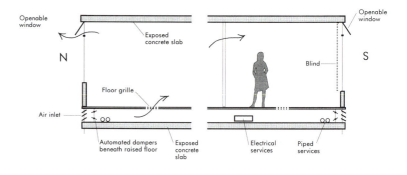

Figure 6.9
Bowling green ventilation strategy

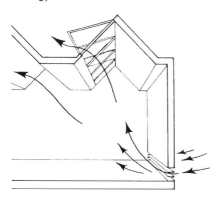

PVs and the natural ventilation strategy

The need to provide conference room facilities in the visitors centre and offices area and future flexibility led to a strategy of a raised floor for services and air distribution as indicated in Figure 6.8.

The bowling green ventilation strategy (Figure 6.9) was developed to both ventilate the internal space and take the heat away from the back of the PV modules to prevent a layer of hot air forming at high level.

The architect considered a variety of wall constructions and favoured, on grounds of appearance and functional performance, a rainscreen cladding system. As this was also perfectly suited to PV panels on the front facade of the bowling green it was chosen.

Choice of module

For the building the architect chose an elegant white steel frame with green rainscreen cladding panels. Monocrystalline modules were selected on the basis of cost and an appearance which complemented that of the building.

Sizing and costing

The design was reviewed and it was decided to adopt the bowling green south facade shown in Figure 6.10. This allowed 60m^2 of PV modules on the facade or 8.8kWp.

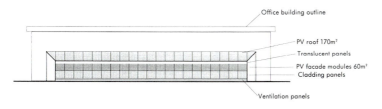

Figure 6.10
South elevation

On the roof using the basic design of Figure 6.7(c) it was possible to put in 114m^2 of PV modules per saw-tooth or 16.8kWp. It was decided to have PVs on the front roof and the upper half of the second saw-tooth as well as the south facade, thus giving a total of 34kWp or about 23kW on a sunny June afternoon (the output is slightly lower than the 25kW aimed for because of the reduced performance of the south facade modules). The annual output from this PV installation is shown in Figure 6.5.

Figure 6.11 shows a sketch of the final scheme. Sketches and a rough schematic were sent to manufacturers for review, costing and an analysis of the output. The manufacturers were asked to keep in mind the client's intention to expand the installation in the future.

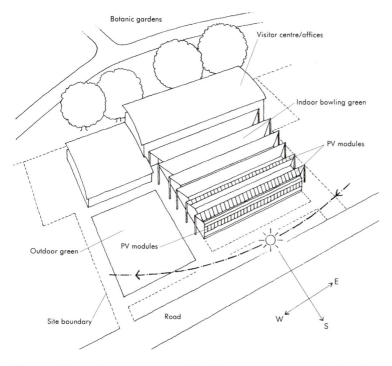

Figure 6.11
Final scheme

The manufacturers' responses varied and some quotes were higher than initial estimates. It was decided to proceed optimistically and use the £150,000 figure cited above and an expected output of 25,000kWh/y. Although no detailed analysis was carried out, rough checks indicated that we would be in Zone A of Figure 4.3.

System considerations

The preliminary PV system design assumed that the PVs would be split into sub-arrays each with its own inverter and that the incoming electrical supply, main switchgear, meters, power conditioners and various data, communications and control panels would all be located in the electrical switchgear room.

Figure 6.12 shows a schematic of the system at this preliminary design stage.

Starting at the mains incomer there is a three phase and neutral cable. Two meters are included in the schematic (however, this is subject to discussion with the electricity supplier). There are four PCUs (each with their own maximum power point tracker) included, each rated at approximately 7kW. One PCU is for the vertical south facade which will receive less irradiation than the PVs mounted on the inclined roofs. The remaining three PCUs have been included in order to modularise the system based upon sub-arrays of equal area.

Each sub-array has five strings and each string has eight modules. The modules are connected together so that each string operates at a system voltage of 280V. The voltage was kept reasonably low for safety. Sub-array termination boxes, approximately 0.5m × 0.5m × 0.2m, are housed at high level in the bowling green at the east end of each sub-array. The sub-array termination boxes are then connected back to the appropriate inverter, thus reducing the number of cables running through the bowling green. The sub-array termination boxes contain isolation switches for individual strings, blocking diodes for the strings, DC fuses and testing points. Good access was provided to the roof to allow for cleaning of the modules and the northlight windows, for maintenance of the opening light mechanisms, and for inspection of all electrics.

Planning the PV installation inside the building

The architect wanted to know:

- The size and the position of the plant room.
- Where the cables were going to run.
- How big they were.

The mechanical and electrical plant rooms were both positioned just to the north of the north-east corner of the indoor bowling hall to allow for ventilation for the boilers and the PV switchgear room (Figure 6.13). This fairly central position, although distant from the first PV modules, was thought to be appropriate over the life of the building when other PV sub-arrays will be positioned much closer to it. It was also thought that if more space for PV equipment became necessary in the future it could come from the adjacent storeroom.

In the electrical switchgear room, approximately 40m² is required for standard equipment and approximately 10m² of additional space is required for PV related equipment. Thus, the PV plant floor area is about 4–5% of the total array area.

All cables were run internally mainly within the supporting framework.

In the indoor bowling hall, cables run to the plant room from the sub-array termination boxes within two compartment trunking (50mm × 100mm overall) elegantly concealed at high level. The eight cables are each approximately 15mm overall diameter.

**Figure 6.12
System schematic**

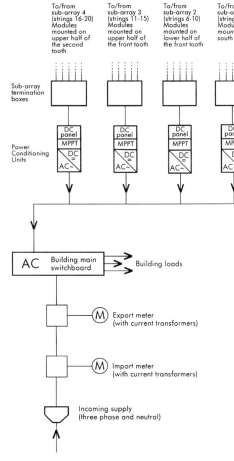

Note: Earthing arrangements not shown

6.4   Future detailed design

It was anticipated that the detailed design stage would address the following points:

- A roof construction detail that would allow for easy substitution of PV modules for metal sheeting.
- Design of the office roof to allow incorporation of PV modules.
- Bonding and lightning protection.

6.5   Project data

Table 6.1 summarises the principal data including cost and performance predictions.

Table 6.1
Data summary

Building

- Floor area (m^2)   3950
- Electrical demand (kWh/y)   137000

PV System	Roof	South facade	Aggregate
• Nominal array rating (kWp)	25.2	8.8	34.0
• Area of PVs (m^2)	170	60	230
• System rating			
(W/m^2 (array)	110	80	102
(W/m^2 (floor area) a	–	–	6
• Assumed performance ratio	0.75	0.75	0.75
• Solar energy available to array (kWh/y)	193000	48500	241500
• Total electrical energy provided by PV system (kWh/y)	20000	5000	25000
• Estimated energy use on site (kWh/y) a	–	–	22,500
• Total avoided CO$_2$ emissions per year due to PV installation (kg)	12400	3100	15500
• Estimated installed cost of PV system (£) a	–	–	150000

a The aggregate total figure has not been separated into components

REFERENCE

1. For the purposes of this book the authors have simplified the building in numerous ways and developed their own cost estimates based on this. In the description of the later stages we have imagined how the design team, client and other parties might have reacted because the actual process had not progressed that far – we freely admit an element of "informed" poetic licence in the chapter.

PROJECT PRINCIPALS

Client:	The Botanic Garden of the University of Cambridge
Architect:	Saunders Boston
Environmental Engineers:	Max Fordham & Partners

7

Solar village at Amersfoort, Holland

Bill Watts and Randall Thomas

7.1   Introduction

Amersfoort is a new development in Holland about 55km from Amsterdam. It is very much under construction as is evident from some of the figures below. From the air it is a disc of new urban development set in a flat, featureless agricultural landscape (see Figure 7.1(a)). From this view it can be seen that in part of the area the roofs are blue, indicated by a dashed line in Figure 7.1(b). It is with pride that Mr Pos of REMU, the local electricity utility, states that this is because most of the houses in this area have substantial PV arrays on the roof.

Figure 7.1(a)
Aerial view of houses in Nieuwland, Amersfoort

7.1(b)
Area of PV roofs

The Dutch government and the electricity companies have agreed on reductions of CO_2 emissions. One result of this is a strategy for the supply of 3.2% of electricity to come from sustainable sources.

At Amersfoort there are a number of initiatives, including the 1MW PV project in the Waterkwartier district which consists of installing more than 12,000m² of modules on 500 houses and a number of public utility buildings.

It is expected that the annual production will be 1,000,000kWh, equivalent to the average electricity consumption of 300 Dutch households.

In addition to reducing CO_2 emissions the goals of the project are (1):

- To illustrate the impact of using solar power at district level.
- To reduce costs by applying solar power on a large scale.
- To illustrate possible management arrangements.
- To acquire know-how and experience regarding electrical engineering and architectural aspects.
- To increase the acceptance of solar-power applications by local authorities, urban development specialists, project developers, housing associations, architects, contractors and residents.

7.2   The development

There is a mixture of private house ownership and ownership by REMU. The PV roofs, however, are financed and owned by REMU who effectively sell it to the householders over 20 years through a leasing arrangement. All the electricity generated by the PVs is credited to the owners whether or not they use it.

A variety of architects were commissioned to create a range of designs (see Figures 7.2–7.11) within a town plan framework that not only included roads and pavements but also waterways. Since PVs work best pointing south the designers had to respond to this constraint. By and large the streets run north–south and east–west. But the methods of incorporating the PVs into the buildings vary markedly from large extrovert displays to subtle, barely noticeable integration.

Figure 7.2
PV modules on roofs (on homes to the left)

Figure 7.3
PV modules on roof of a school

Figure 7.4
PV modules on roof

Figure 7.5
PV modules on the roof of the Energy Balance Home (and some opening windows)

Figure 7.6
Free-standing PV modules on roofs, one
dumper-truck and a pony

The massing often seems constrained to present the right and precise angles for the modules. An indication of this is given in Figure 7.7 showing the north-facing rear of a group of homes.

Figure 7.7
Rear view of a group of PV homes

For anyone who knows the cost of PVs the use of them at times appears a bit extravagant. Separate steel structures holding an (albeit elegant) array over the road as an architectural device to complete a square (Figure 7.8)

Figure 7.8
Steel bridging structures with PV arrays

may appear somewhat excessive to a UK observer. However, it is accepted that there is a balance to be struck between utilitarian considerations and those of spatial planning form.

The houses are expensive and in demand. The new owners tend to have young families. This is registered in the number of new primary schools in the area, again with PV roofs. The planners have realised that they have a bulge of infants to deal with, which will disappear as the population matures. To allow for this they have put primary schools into new houses (with tiled PV roofs) in the expectation that they will later become dwellings (Figure 7.9).

Figure 7.9
PV roofs on a building currently used as a school

At the sports centre PVs are part of the roof (Figure 7.10) and also form the canopy over the ubiquitous bike racks (Figure 7.11).

Figure 7.10
Sports centre with PVs on the roof and on the bike shelter

7.3 The Energy Balance Home

The REMU showhouse which is shown in Figure 7.5 is termed "The Energy Balance Home". REMU's objectives were to:

- Stimulate sustainable, low-energy, residential construction and the use of renewable energy.
- Acquire experience with solar power systems linked to the mains.
- Collect data on the production and use of energy in these homes and to make the data known to other parties initiating action in this area.
- Acquire knowledge concerning combinations of new energy techniques.

Figure 7.11
Close-up of bike shelter

The design of the Energy Balance Homes is based on three principles: reduction of energy consumption, use of renewable energy and use of building materials from renewable sources.

The construction of the Energy Balance Homes was co-ordinated by a construction team consisting of REMU and the two architects. A separate "roof-integration working group" was created for integration of the solar-energy systems, consisting of REMU, the architects, the consultants, the suppliers of solar collectors and solar cells and the supplier of the aluminium sections.

The $160m^2$ roof has $93m^2$ of PV modules. Most of these modules are opaque, but some consist of PVs on a glass substrate which lets some light through. Part of the roof is clear glass and part has $14m^2$ of solar thermal panels. Energy from the solar thermal panels is used both for domestic hot water (DHW) and for space heating. The latter is done in connection with an electric heat pump using refrigerant R407C. Thermal energy storage is in a 300l cylinder for DHW, a 500l cylinder for space heating and in the groundwater layer at a depth of about 12m for long term storage.

The energy balance of the house is given in Table 7.1.

Table 7.1
Energy Balance Home demand and supply statistics

	Demand kWh		Supply kWh
Small power	2200	PVs	7500
Lighting	800	Solar thermal panels	2500
Equipment (pumps, DHW heater)	500	Passive solar	1500
Ventilation	4000	Reclaimed heat	3000
		Internal heat gains	2000
Heating	5000		
DHW	4000		
Total	16500	Total	16500

The PV strings operate at 64 volts DC; this becomes 230V AC at the inverters (Mastervolt type Sunmaster 1800).

As REMU are sponsors of the scheme they are happy to buy and sell energy at the same price. Thus, it is possible to simplify the metering arrangements and use only one.

7.4   Conclusion

Amersfoort is an exceptionally encouraging example of forward thinking. It addresses issues of urban planning, aesthetics, environmental engineering and economics. It is one of the few large-scale examples of planning for photovoltaics and serves as a test-bed and inspiration to us all.

REFERENCE

1.   (Undated). Anon. Two semi-detached Energy-Balance Homes. Description available from REMU, The Renewable Energy Information Centre, Nieuwlandsweg 42, Amersfoort, The Netherlands.

WEBSITE

1.   A Website is in preparation.

Parkmount Housing, Belfast

Richard Partington

8.1   Introduction

With the prospect of peace Belfast is enjoying rejuvenation and housing schemes are springing up all around. But housing is a contentious issue in Northern Ireland. Neighbourhoods earmarked for redevelopment resist to protect sectarian and territorial boundaries, private investors steer clear of the derelict and threatening no-go areas, and consultation processes can be long and drawn out. As a result there has been little scope for innovation and new development has been conventional and cautious. Parkmount (see Figure 8.1) is one of several projects underway in the city that is helping to reverse the trend. The scheme will provide modern, energy-efficient and healthy homes for young and low-income households. A principal aim is to make good use of solar energy.

Figure 8.1
Sketch view of entrance

The scheme is developing in parallel with an urban design study that will look beyond the site boundaries to consider the neighbouring streets and public spaces and possible improvements to public transport. The scheme will in part be publicly funded to initiate a wider program of renewal in the area and to demonstrate that best-practice elements and real innovation can be incorporated in housing for sale on the open market.

8.2   Project history

In 1997 The Northern Ireland Housing Executive, the main public body responsible for delivering housing, established a project team to promote new ideas in housing design with the intention of building these into a demonstration project. Their own technical team sought contributions from academic bodies and specialist companies, and pursued three themes: the possibilities of low-energy design in urban housing; the connection between built form and health and well-being; and flexible dwellings that accommodate changing patterns of use and occupation.

A prototype scheme, called Home Building 2000, aimed to raise public awareness of housing design and was used to make preliminary applications for grant funding. A suitable site was identified and the NIHE then looked to private developers, through a tender process, to deliver the project and take the risk for marketing and sales.

The Carvill Group, a family based company with a portfolio of work in Northern Ireland, Dublin, Glasgow and Berlin, won the tender and commissioned the work described in this section. With their consultant team in place they set about defining a brief and agreeing with the NIHE realistic standards that could be used to judge the scheme. There was a process of negotiation and discussion that clarified at the outset the aims of all the parties. Sketch proposals were made and reviewed and within a very short period an outline design was developed. Further consultations then took place with the planners, local politicians, the highways authority and the funding bodies.

8.3   Brief

The accommodation will consist of 56 two-bedroom apartments (approximately 60m^2) with four smaller one-bedroom apartments. The detailed brief will evolve as grant applications are submitted and research opportunities arise. However, the key components are:

*   Flexible apartment plans to anticipate changes in work patterns and lifestyles.
*   Creation of a defined "place" with landscaping and safe play areas.
*   A completely secure development with controlled access.
*   A logical sequence for marketing and constructing the scheme in phased stages to limit the financial risk.
*   Simple and reliable technical solutions that will be economic to run and maintain.
*   Attainment of the BRE Environmental Standard Award "Homes for a Greener World".
*   Good design for maximising solar potential with a high research and innovation component centred around the use of PVs.

The project achieves a relatively high density of up to 450 rooms per hectare (180 habitable rooms per acre) of useable area and takes on board the ideas recently promoted by the Urban Task Force for renewing our cities and towns (1).

8.4   The site

The site is a long, thin strip of derelict land, aligned on a north–south axis, two miles from the centre of Belfast. A flat area in the centre approximately 35 metres wide and 150 metres long provides the only useful space to build upon. Figure 8.2 shows the site.

Along its eastern edge, where a row of semi-detached houses previously stood, there is a continuous frontage to Shore Road, which historically was a main route north out of Belfast and is still a busy multi-lane highway. To the west the land rises very steeply in a densely wooded escarpment. From the top, nearly eight metres above the road, there are dramatic views of Belfast Lough, the Harland and Wolf dockyards with their twin yellow cranes, and the city centre.

Figure 8.2
The existing site

The woodland and western escarpment rises up to approximately eight metres above the building level and there will be some overshadowing from the trees on the west side of the site in late evening during the summer months.

8.5 External environment and site strategy

The design team began to investigate layouts that would maximise solar potential, considering daylighting, passive solar gain and the use of PVs. We looked at courtyard forms that grouped buildings around an enclosed landscaped space, creating a haven from the busy road. We compared these layouts with designs based on separate towers – good for solar orientation but by their "object-like" nature less useful for defining space. Figure 8.3a–c shows some of our sketch ideas for grouping buildings.

Figure 8.3a
Sketch ideas for grouping buildings

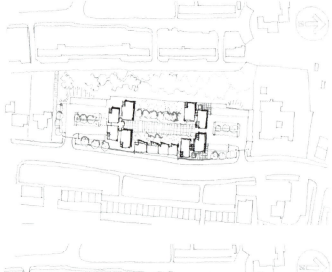

Figure 8.3b
Sketch ideas for grouping buildings

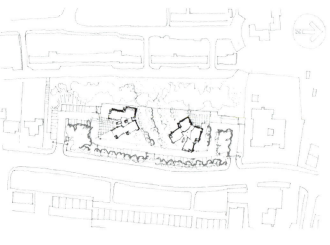

Figure 8.3c
Sketch ideas for grouping buildings

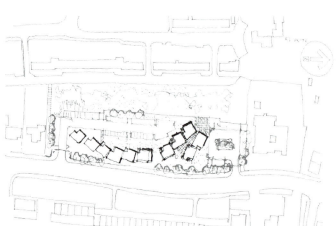

The scheme that emerged from these discussions places a tall building (eight storeys) at the north end of the site with a gently curving arc of lower buildings starting with a two-storey block at the southern end. The ascending heights of the buildings ensure that each mono-pitch roof presents a large area to the southern sky for an efficient PV installation without overshadowing from adjacent buildings in the scheme. With this arrangement the views from an existing terrace of houses at the east of the site are also preserved. Figure 8.4 shows the developed layout. Figure 8.5 shows an aerial view of the developed site layout.

The design team was nervous about this layout. We thought it looked expensive, because of the tower and the large wall area created, and we considered leaving it out of our feasibility proposals. But the client could see benefits that had not occurred to us. The layout makes good sense from a commercial and marketing standpoint – generally house builders prefer to build in phases so that early sales can fund the latter stages. By starting at

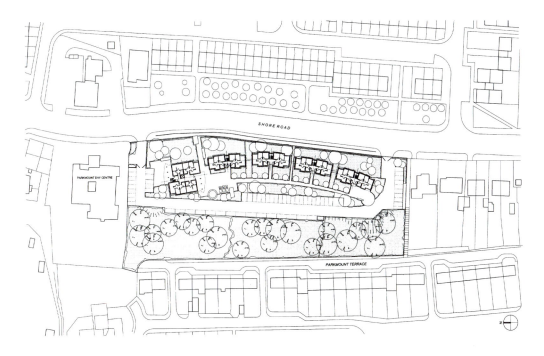

Figure 8.4
The developed site layout

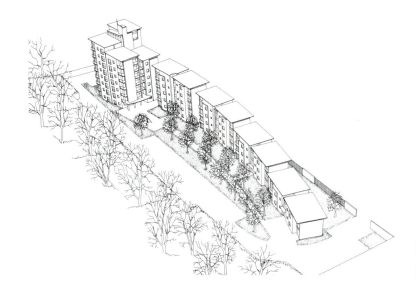

Figure 8.5
Aerial view of the developed site layout.

the southern end and building up the developer will avoid the higher-risk construction of the tower (concrete frame and piled foundations) until marketing and sales are well underway.

More than 80% of the apartments have good orientation for sunlight and many have dual aspect living rooms. Those that do not, because of the density and the constrained site, have the compensation of the best views in a north–east direction towards the Lough. Figure 8.6 shows an analysis of daylighting.

Figure 8.6
Daylighting analysis

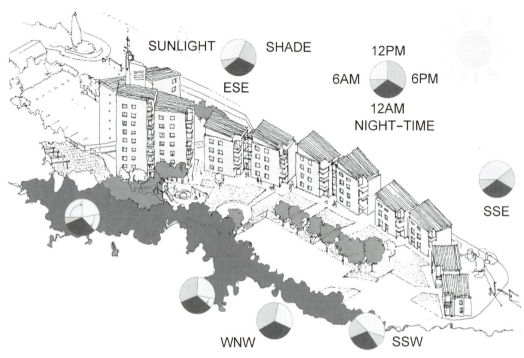

8.6 Monitoring

Two of the apartment buildings have similar orientations and the same number of apartments. It is proposed that one of these will incorporate experimental technology, such as rainwater recycling and a conservatory/thermal buffer device with solar mass storage. The other building will act as a control block incorporating best-practice elements as for the rest of the scheme. The Department of the Built Environment at Ulster University, Belfast will undertake the monitoring of the buildings.

8.7 Photovoltaic panels – strategy

All of the buildings, except the tower, have roofs that are designed to slope gently southwards at a suitable angle for the future installation of photovoltaic panels. A pilot installation, with an array of 10m^2 of photovoltaic panels on the roof of the tower was originally proposed. This would provide sufficient energy for lighting in the common areas (lift lobby or stairway).

A larger array of 70m^2 is now being designed with an estimated annual output of 4400kWh, which should provide ample electricity to meet the annual consumption of two of the apartments. The design for this roof will be applicable to all the low-rise units in the future.

Three important issues have been considered in the roof design:

- How to maintain an effective waterproof layer that is not compromised by the PV installation.
- Design for future retrofitted panels without complete replacement of the roof.
- Access for maintenance and cleaning and future installation.

We began to research comparable installations where the PV array and the roof covering had been integrated seamlessly to form a continuous surface (rather than being added as an afterthought). We were already familiar with PV products being marketed to look like traditional tiling or that interlock with common clay or concrete tiles. None of these, however, satisfied our aim of promoting and celebrating the technology. We also had concerns about the design of the junction between the PV panels and traditional roof coverings where there could be a potential weakness in the waterproofing. It is often at the interface between trades where failures occur – in this case between the roof "fixer" and the specialist PV installer. Our preliminary investigations clarified one underlying challenge for the project – how to introduce a precisely engineered, and technically sophisticated product within the culture and limitations of housing construction and house builders.

We considered the possibility that PV panels might be installed on roofs in 10–20 years' time when improvements in manufacture and external pressures (government incentives or CO_2 taxation) will make PVs cost-effective. The roofs have an orientation and slope that take account of this but the life expectancy of most pitched roofing materials exceeds 20 years so we have tried to devise a solution that allows an installation to be laid over an existing roof covering leaving the waterproofing intact, a rain-screen in effect. Design work has concentrated on achieving an acceptable architectural appearance using this approach.

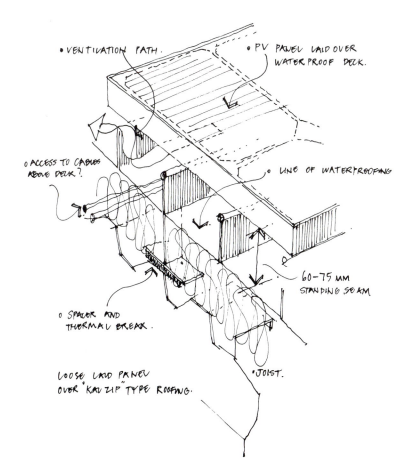

Figure 8.7
Sketch of panel and roof covering

Safety and access also have to be carefully considered. Where there are multiple tenancies or households under one roof – social housing, housing for rent – the common or landlord services are usually physically separated from the tenants. Access and servicing of all the installation and wiring needs to be on the landlord "side" and the logical position of the wiring from the panels is therefore above the roof, ie externally. This is a further reason for treating the PV installation as a rain-screen rather than integrating it with the covering. The DC wiring in the vertical risers would also be contained in separate trunking to isolate it from the domestic wiring. Figure 8.7 shows the relationship of the PV panels to the roof covering, with an indication of the ventilation path.

The roof itself will use either profiled aluminium or the better looking but more expensive standing-seam type sheet material. There are three reasons for choosing a metal roof:

*   Economy – sheet aluminium roofs are cheap to install and can be recycled.
*   Technology – there is already available a large body of products and knowledge developed around secondary fixings and securing devices (for safety harnesses access etc.).
*   Opportunity – there is enormous solar potential in the huge acreage of industrial roofs that exist on factories and out-of-town sheds.

Sheet metal roofs are produced in huge volumes and many manufacturers have devised ingenious systems for fixing brackets and penetrations to or through the roof covering. Unlike slate or tiled roofs which overlap the fixings to achieve water-tightness the sheets themselves are fixed with exposed external fixings so the roofing technology can be more readily adapted to support the PV panels above.

8.8   Photovoltaic panels – detailed development

PV development is moving at a quick pace and even in the short lifespan of this project we have found that many of the products used in the built schemes that we studied have been improved. Recent advances have introduced thinner "films" for the conducting layer in thin film panels, reducing the overall thickness to 7 or 8mm; in other words, the thickness of a sheet of laminated glass. In this type of thin film panel semiconductor alloys (amorphous silicon and amorphous silicon germanium) are deposited in thin layers on glass.

Manufacturers have also devised ways of bonding photovoltaic cells to flat-roof type single-ply roofing membranes. Some products have flexible PV cells laminated to the waterproof membrane in the factory and the whole system is delivered to site in roll form ready to be laid out over the supporting deck. Figure 8.8 shows a comparison of panel arrangements.

Thin film PV modules like BP's Millennia series are about half as efficient as the highest rated monocrystalline panels but they are approximately one-quarter of the cost. Their performance is less variable with temperature and they are tolerant of both shading and higher operating temperatures, in theory reducing the ventilation requirements. We have been attracted to thin film technology because of the lower costs, albeit with a trade off in efficiency (see Table 8.1). Our design thinking has also shifted – we are now designing with something more like a sheet of glass rather than a panel with an ugly edge surround and a visible thickness. Furthermore, all of the proprietary bolt-through and "planar" type fixings will be compatible with thin film glass panels allowing for elegant and clean-lined attachments of panels to their supporting structures. Figure 8.9 shows possible fixing details. These are important visual issues in our scheme, which will be viewed from above as well as from the street. We think that the roof scape needs to be treated as a "fifth" elevation.

Table 8.1
Panel data (2)

Panel type	Relative efficiency %	Output kWh/m²/y	Material cost (comparative) £/m²
Monocrystalline	100	118	400
Polycrystalline	88	104	350
Thin film	55	65	110

Work is progressing on a roof edge detail that projects above the waterproof covering sufficiently to hide the under supports of the glass PVs but aligns with the top surface to give a completely smooth surface. The same edge profile will be used on all the roofs, forming a coping, to allow panels to be added progressively over time. The supporting structure for the PVs can be a simple framework of galvanised steel sections to which safety harnesses for maintenance will also fix. Access to the roofs and inverters will be gained directly from the central core with vertical risers incorporated within the stair enclosure.

The array will be connected to the national grid and so any electricity provided in surplus of on-site requirements can be used elsewhere. In preliminary discussions Northern Ireland Electricity have indicated their support for the project and one of the aims will be to secure an agreement to connect to the national grid – although this may not be straightforward because the array output is comparatively small (3). A two-way metering system would be prohibitively expensive and, in general, the electricity providers are reluctant to service and administer the metering of small-scale

Figure 8.8
Comparison of panel arrangements
(a) Mechanically fixed PV panels:
• PV cells on glass units fixed to standing seam roofing system.
• Weight of PV panels and fixing mechanisms: 20kg/m².
• Maximum PV area: 72m².
• Central access zone for cleaning maintenance required.
• Annual output: 62kWh/m²/year. (Total: 4464kWh/year)
• Supply cables taken over roof parapet to inverters located in service core area.

(b) Bonded PV panels:
• PV cells factory bonded to single ply roofing membrane rolls 1.05m wide.
• Weight of installation including roof membrane: 4kg/m².
• Maximum PV area: 56.5m².
• No special zones for access required as membrane tolerant of light foot traffic.
• Annual output: 45–53kWh/m²/year. (Total: 2552–2993kWh/year)
• Supply cables wired to back of each panel and fed through roof deck to inverters in roof void below.

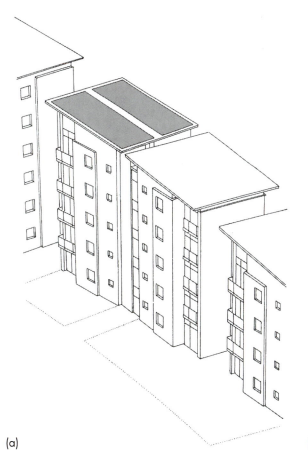

(a)

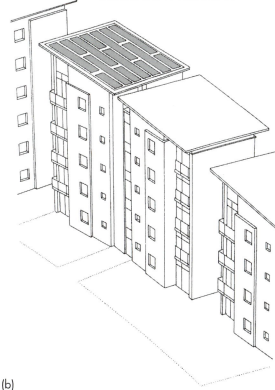

(b)

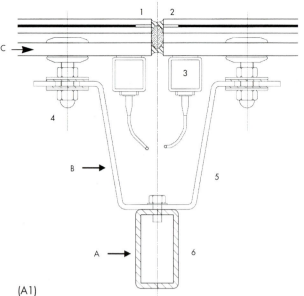

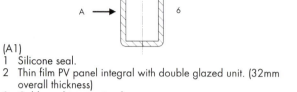

(A1)

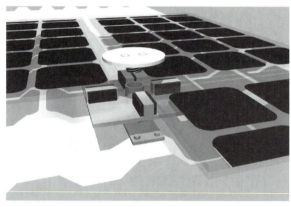

(A2)

1 Silicone seal.
2 Thin film PV panel integral with double glazed unit. (32mm overall thickness)
3 Cable and termination box.
4 Proprietary bolt through fixing with captive bolt.
5 Support legs.
6 Structure (80 × 50mm Rectangular hollow section).

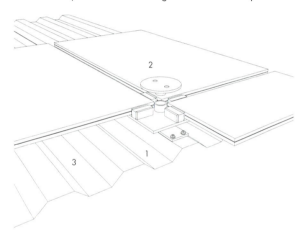

(B1)

1 Fixing bracket bolted through deck to sub-structure.
2 Custom made edge support and retaining cap (60mm diameter stainless steel).
3 Ventilation gap under panels (approx. 50mm).

(B2)

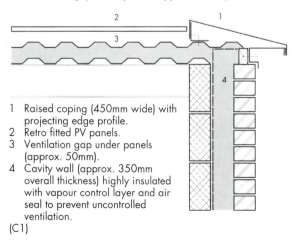

1 Raised coping (450mm wide) with projecting edge profile.
2 Retro fitted PV panels.
3 Ventilation gap under panels (approx. 50mm).
4 Cavity wall (approx. 350mm overall thickness) highly insulated with vapour control layer and air seal to prevent uncontrolled ventilation.

(C1)

(C2)

Figure 8.9
Fixing details

projects. We would like to see a credit system whereby the installation's estimated output would be deducted from the annual consumption (the estimated output will be checked against monitored output). This would be an interim measure until two-way metering became more widespread.

The scheme has further potential – the large mono-pitch roofs could be used for combining PVs with a rainwater recycling system, housing the water tanks in parts of the roof void. This may be an area for research on later phases or on a future project, as well as the possibility of opening up the space under the sloping roof to create highly desirable "lofts", with galleries, on the top floor apartments.

8.9   Summary

The project is progressing from outline to scheme design, and the incorporation of PVs has required detailed consideration and co-ordination at an early stage in the process. There has been a necessary adjustment in the sequence of decision-making and, for a speculative house developer, a much earlier commitment to development work and consultants' fees.

Housing schemes often progress through planning with minimal design input (architects are often only used to smooth the planning process). Housing developers, working to very tight margins, may be reluctant to engage in the level of development discussion that a PV installation demands and few would contemplate the preliminary research and development that was undertaken on the Doxford project described in Chapter 10. Ingenuity and invention is required to integrate the PV installation architecturally. This has to be paid for, but as planning authorities are looking favourably on schemes that demonstrate a commitment to renewable resources the benefits of PVs may soon be recognised by house builders. Parkmount is a demonstration project for a progressive and enthusiastic client but the client is unusual in this respect and has been prepared to work on development proposals, grant applications and design presentations to establish the scheme.

Although the PV installation is relatively small we have found that thinking ahead to ensure that we maximise the future potential of the technology has clearly influenced the scheme both technically and architecturally. PVs have influenced the site strategy, the layout, form and appearance of the buildings. Figures 8.10 and 8.11 show the developed proposals prepared for planning. As the first urban housing scheme in Northern Ireland to incorporate photovoltaics Parkmount will be a significant technical and visual landmark, setting a standard for future speculative and non-commercial development.

Figure 8.10
Scheme submitted for planning consent:
elevation

Figure 8.11
Scheme submitted for planning consent:
perspective

REFERENCES

1.   "Towards an Urban Renaissance", Final Report of the Urban Task Force, E&FN Spon, 1999.
2.   Private communication, BP Solarex, February 2000.
3.   A good account of the obstacles that prevent grid connection and selling back to the provider is given in Appendix D of the ETSU account of the Roaf House: Roaf, S. and Fuentes, M. (1999). Demonstration Project for a 4KW Domestic Photovoltaic Roof in Oxford. ETSU S/P2/00236/REP. ETSU: Harwell.

PROJECT PRINCIPALS

Client: The Carvill Group
Architect: Richard Partington Architects
Urban Design: Llewelyn-Davies
Environmental Engineers: Max Fordham & Partners
Quantity Surveyor: The Carvill Group

The Charter School

Randall Thomas

9.1   Introduction

The Charter School, Dulwich, London is a new school which is being established in existing educational premises (constructed in 1956–57 using a system-built approach). Such buildings are typical of many in the UK (and elsewhere) and as such offer an exceptional opportunity to develop ways of upgrading a significant percentage of the existing building stock. Figure 9.1 shows a site plan of the school with the rectilinear arrangement all too typical of these developments. Design work on redevelopment started in June 1999.

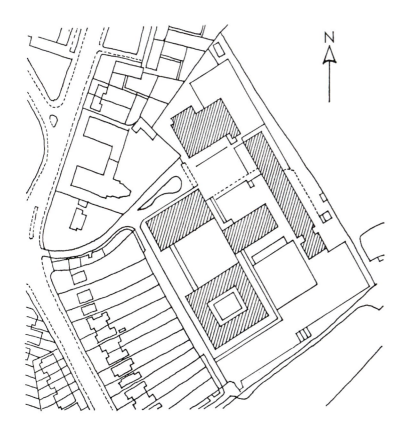

N

Figure 9.1
Site plan

The project was the subject of a competition to select an architect who would "provide a sensitive and exciting modern design with an identity appropriate for a secondary school with a broadly defined access policy where pupils have high ambitions for educational achievement in the 21st century". In responding to this, the winning design team, led by Penoyre & Prasad Architects with environmental design advice from Max Fordham & Partners chose to propose a number of sustainable approaches to the refurbishment (discussed below) and to use photovoltaics as part of a new roof covering an existing courtyard. PVs were seen as a way of symbolising the scientific and progressive ideas of the School as well as providing an excellent pedagogical device for increasing environmental awareness. The incorporation of PVs in the competition entry enhanced the strength of the submission.

9.2   Site

Dulwich is a leafy suburb in south-east London. The topography gently undulates and behind the larger houses one imagines John Betjeman's tennis players engaged in a not-too-strenuous game. The site of the school is mainly flat with slight changes of level being taken up by flights of three or four steps; the total site area is 20,260m². The principal axis of the site runs approximately north–west/south–east. To the south-west of the site is two-storey housing and to the north-east playing fields. Trees are mainly located around the perimeter, although a number are in the courtyards and open spaces between the buildings.

9.3   Buildings

Classrooms, science and arts facilities, an administrative block, a hall, a kitchen, a gymnasium – all the structures of a modern educational establishment are here, but lack of maintenance and a number of insensitive additions to a rather elegant architectural vocabulary, derived in part from Mies van der Rohe, have left the school with a slightly tired feeling (Figures 9.2, 9.3 and 9.4).

Figure 9.2
Entrance to the hall

Figure 9.3
Elevation of Science block

Figure 9.4
Courtyard (showing relatively recent new roofing)

The client, Southwark Education and the School Board of Governors, was well aware of this and in the brief called for creative architectural and design work to create an "attractive and welcoming" institution and one which provided a high-quality environment with low future maintenance costs and high levels of energy efficiency.

At present the insulation levels are poor, windows are all single-glazed and the buildings are inadequately sealed. These issues are all being addressed in the refurbishment of the school. The intention is to upgrade the fabric by replacing deteriorating cladding over, say, the next 10 years.

Records of energy consumption indicate that energy use in the past was approximately $360kWh/m^2/y$ for space and water heating from gas-fired boilers (data for electricity use was unfortunately not available). There was scope for improvement.

9.4   Environmental strategy

A broad environmental strategy study was carried out.

The goal was to set out a range of possibilities which would enable the School to become a national example of environmentally responsible refurbishment of high architectural quality over the next 20 years. A long-term goal, perhaps for beyond the year 2020, was a school that over the course of a year produced more energy (probably through photovoltaics (PV) panels) than it used.

Site considerations such as the creation of favourable microclimates and rainwater use were examined. Great emphasis was placed upon maximising the solar potential of the site, concentrating on the use of daylighting to reduce energy consumption for artificial lighting, passive solar gain to reduce the space heating requirement and photovoltaics to provide electricity on site.

Our initial assessment was that the potential area available for PVs was 80 to 90% of the total roof area. Figure 9.5 shows the basic block arrangements, with areas likely to be suitable for PVs shaded.

The generous spacing of the buildings and the overall massing with the taller three-storey science block to the north-east led us to an initial quick assessment which was quite optimistic. But when we started to look more closely at the roofs with their water storage tank enclosures, extract fans and daylights (see Figure 9.6) we became more cautious about the potential for

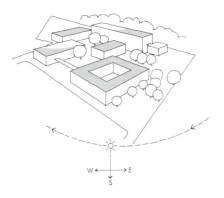

Figure 9.5
Roofs potentially suitable for PVs

Figure 9.6
Detail of roof obstructions

photovoltaic panels. This came as something of a surprise to us and highlights the need for a detailed study of accessible, unshaded area even on spacious suburban sites.

If we conservatively assume that 50% of the existing roof area of 4600m^2 is suitable for PVs, and using our rule-of-thumb of 100kWh/m^2/y gives a total supply of approximately 230,000kWh/y. A very approximate estimate of electrical energy consumption in a completely refurbished site is 210,000kWh/y, thus PVs could meet all of this figure (in practice most of this energy would be used on site but some would be exported to the grid).

In the course of developing the design, the possibility of collecting rainwater was considered and incorporated. Rainwater from the new courtyard roof will be stored below ground in three connected 7.7m^3 storage tanks. From these it will be pumped to a header tank above the four-storey building lift shaft for use in flushing WCs and urinals.

Where space is available, future developments could include collecting rainwater and transferring it directly to holding tanks in roof spaces or on the upper floors for use for flushing. The idea would be to avoid taking the water down to ground level and then pumping it back up to high level.

Building considerations

Figure 9.7
Summary of environmental
considerations

Figure 9.7 summarises the main environmental considerations for the facade and section. Of particular importance for PVs is the ample daylighting and the high-efficiency artificial lighting.

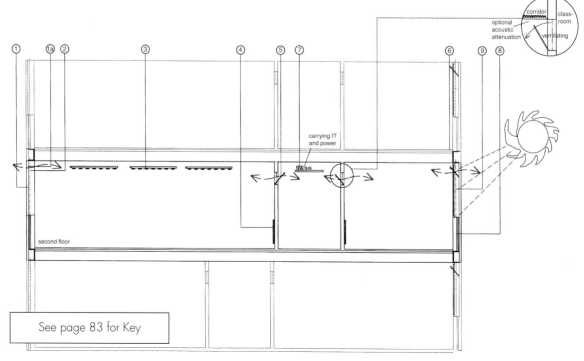

See page 83 for Key

Key to figure 9.7

Typical cross-section of an existing block showing new environmental services integration up to the year 2020. It is assumed that the school will be in use for 11 months of the year – therefore night cooling will be required during the summer months.

1.   All windows equipped with high performance glazing, eg triple glazing.
1a.   Glazing with low emissivity coating.
2.   Trickle ventilators for semi-controlled fresh air supply.
3.   High-efficiency lighting.
4.   Small radiators.
5.   Openable panel over door for ventilation into corridor if required and in use for night ventilation with optional acoustic attenuation.
6.   Hopper windows, possibly on both sides.
7.   Service runs (at present situated on the perimeter of the building) gathered into zone above corridor suspended ceiling.
8.   Highly insulated replacement cladding.
9.   Horizontal blinds incorporated into triple glazing for solar control.

9.5   The atrium

In the first phase of development a new entrance is being created and an existing courtyard is being covered, in part with PVs to create a stunning atrium (see Figure 9.8).

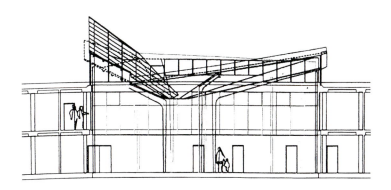

Figure 9.8
Section showing atrium roof

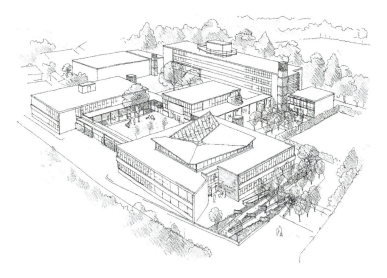

Figure 9.9
The atrium roof in the context of the site

The major PV design input has focused on the atrium, which was seen to be multipurpose with uses varying from meetings to exhibitions. Ample daylight was essential. The temperature needed to be at least 15°C and, preferably, 18 to 20°C in winter. In the summer it was important that the space not overheat. To allow for both daylighting and photovoltaics it was decided to put the PV panels on the part of the roof indicated in Figure 9.10.

Figure 9.10
Atrium roof

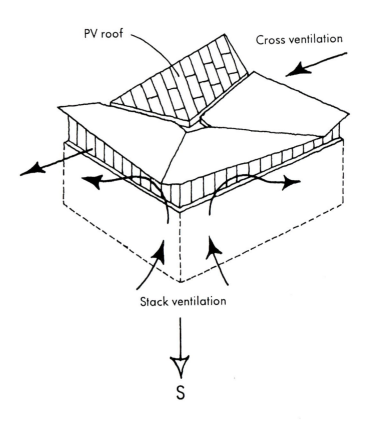

Figure 9.10
Atrium roof

It was evident early on that the ventilation of the atrium and air flow over the back of the PV modules needed to be treated together. Preliminary calculations suggested that at least 10 air changes per hour would be required in the atrium to avoid overheating. A night-time cooling strategy was also essential. Considerable thought was given to how to introduce such large amounts of air into an essentially "land-locked" space. The final solution incorporated bringing in air through ducts above the ground floor false ceiling of the adjacent spaces and above doors. Air then rises through the atrium.

It was thought important to take at least some of the extract air over the backs of the modules to reduce their temperature and improve performance. As is common at this point in the design development the type of module had not been selected and so both crystalline and thin film PVs had to be allowed for.

Acceptable temperatures are realised through a combination of stack effect and cross ventilation at the top of the atrium when the wind is blowing. This is achieved with the aid of horizontal pivot opening windows on all four sides of the atrium (see Figure 9.10).

The annual amount of electricity likely to be available was estimated roughly at an early stage at about 5000kWh using monocrystalline silicon modules.

There was discussion about how this output should be used. It was very important for the client to "prove a tangible use" for the PV-generated electricity. One proposal was to supply a number of classrooms directly, but this was not adopted because it would not have made the best use of the electricity available. Instead it was decided to feed the PVs into the mains and to meter the output. Another meter was proposed to monitor use in the classrooms. Both results would be displayed at a panel in the atrium to provide a continuous indication of the benefits of the installation. Over the next 20 years it was anticipated that additional PV modules would be added to the school and the increased contribution indicated in a similar way.

Design development involved detailed discussions with PV manufacturers. A final decision on module type and area has not yet been made, but the key considerations under review are cost, size of the array and output. Visual appearance is of less importance in choosing between options.

9.6   Conclusion

More examples of the far-sighted approach to energy conservation and supply that the Charter School has taken are needed in the UK. This school should provide a model for the regeneration of a significant part of our building stock, with PVs having an important role to play in this process.

PROJECT PRINCIPALS

Client:	Southwark Education and the Charter School Board of Governors
Architect:	Penoyre & Prasad
Environmental Consultant:	Max Fordham & Partners
Building Services Engineer:	Southwark Building Design Service
Structural Engineer:	Allott and Lomax
Landscape Architect:	Watkins: Dalley
Quantity Surveyor:	Franklin and Andrews

The Solar Office: Doxford International

David Lloyd Jones

10.1 Introduction

The Solar Office (see Figure 10.1) is a new office building designed for Akeler plc on the 32ha Doxford International Business Park, located in Sunderland in the north-east of England. It is occupied by the leading e-commerce company domainnames.com. The brief for the building and its procurement followed the robust fast-track pattern that is now commonplace in speculative office development, a course already adopted and refined at Doxford. Where it breaks with convention is in its response to energy use and the environment.

Figure 10.1
Elevation of the Solar Office from the south

The building is designed to minimise the use of energy while its external fabric, through the incorporation of a photovoltaic array, will provide solar power. This formula for energy self-sufficiency is one of the key building blocks of future global sustainability.

The design addresses all the environmental and energy-conserving issues. The energy-consumption target for the building when occupied by a tenant with conventional power requirements is 85kWh/m²/y compared with a conventional air-conditioned office of over 400kWh/m²/y. Electricity generation is provided by a photovoltaic solar array, integrated into the building envelope. The 73kWp array provides 55,100kWh of electrical energy per annum, which represents between one-third and one-quarter of the electricity expected to be used by the occupants over the period of a year. In summer, when it will generate more than is required, the surplus will be exported to the National Grid.

The Solar Office is the first speculatively constructed office building to incorporate building-integrated photovoltaics, and the resulting solar facade is the largest so far constructed in Europe. It is one of the few to adopt a holistic energy strategy. It achieved an "excellent" BREEAM (Building Research Establishment Environmental Assessment Method) rating. It was selected as a 'Millennium Product' by the Design Council of Great Britain and won the 2000 Eurosolar award.

10.2 The brief

The 4600m² three-storey building was constructed to a "shell and core" specification. It is fitted out to suit the specific requirements of the occupying tenant. The tenant was encouraged to operate the building in its low-energy "passive solar" mode, but chose to augment this strategy by utilising the provision made for "mixed mode" operation since heat emitted from office equipment and the occupants is above average. The building is designed to be robust, versatile and to offer exceptional value. It can, if necessary, be divided into up to six separate tenancies.

The whole building was designed and constructed over 15 months on a design-and-build basis. This means that the contractor is required to construct it within a fixed cost to a fixed delivery date with the consultants novated to the contractor on completion of an approved scheme design.

10.3 The building

Building layout

The building is V-shaped in plan with the extreme ends of the "V" splayed away from each other. A central core is located at the apex of the "V". The building incorporates a 66m-long, south-facing, inclined facade at the centre of which is the main entrance. Behind the facade is located a three-storey atrium and, between the facade and the splayed wings, an internal passageway (see Figures 10.2 and 10.3).

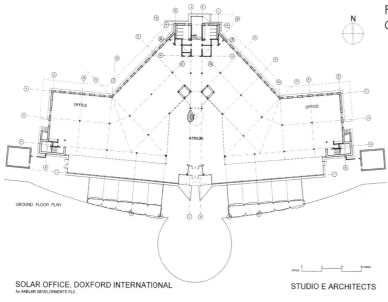

Figure 10.2
Ground floor plan

SOLAR OFFICE, DOXFORD INTERNATIONAL
for AKELER DEVELOPMENTS PLC.

STUDIO E ARCHITECTS

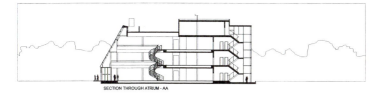

Figure 10.3
Sections

SOLAR OFFICE, DOXFORD INTERNATIONAL
for AKELER DEVELOPMENTS PLC.

STUDIO E ARCHITECTS

Setting back each wing in plan by 5° off south has negligible effect on PV efficiency but does give the long elevation a sculptural and light reflective dynamic. Originally this facade was to be more planar, over-sailing both ends of the building and the roofline. Cost reduction led to the current form. It is still, though, around 950m² in area.

The building and its site

Key site issues were layout, orientation and climate (see Figure 10.4). It was found that the facade could be aligned to face due south and sloped at 60° to the ground, without compromising internal planning. This configuration provides good solar radiation at this northerly latitude. The inclined and sealed facade overcame the potential problems of dazzle and noise from passing traffic on the adjacent trunk road; office windows could be placed facing north, north-east and north-west, obviating the need for elaborate solar protection; and placing the car park in front of the building ensured that the solar facade would not be over-shadowed. The main entrance, being located in the centre of the south facade, requires those approaching to encircle the building's conventional brickwork frontages before revealing its prime feature, the iridescent array.

Figure 10.4
Site plan

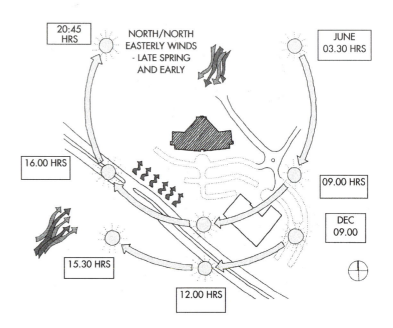

The site, being elevated and close to the sea, is very exposed and therefore subject to strong winds. Care was needed in the detailed design of the openings to ensure the building exploited the beneficial effects of the wind (see below).

10.4 The energy strategy

The overriding objective in terms of the environmental design was to find a synthesis between the low-energy measures and those needed for an effective photovoltaic installation (see Figure 10.5). The low-energy measures include:

- Limited depth floors (maximum 15m) with generous ceiling heights to encourage cross ventilation and good daylighting.
- Provision for secure night ventilation and the exploitation of building structure to provide thermal mass in order to provide night-time cooling in summer.

- Windows which offer good controllable ventilation, glare-free daylight and solar control.
- A well-insulated, impermeable building envelope to minimise heat loss in winter.
- Responsive controls to avoid frustrating the occupants.
- Knowledgeable and sensitive building management.

Figure 10.5
Cut-away perspective

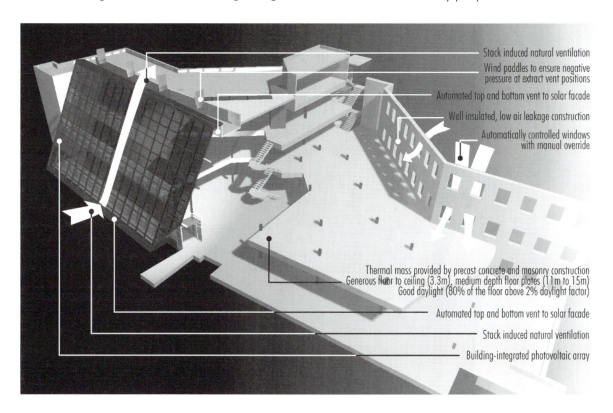

Stack induced natural ventilation
Wind paddles to ensure negative pressure at extract vent positions
Automated top and bottom vent to solar facade
Well insulated, low air leakage construction
Automatically controlled windows with manual override

Thermal mass provided by precast concrete and masonry construction
Generous floor to ceiling (3.3m), medium depth floor plates (11m to 15m)
Good daylight (80% of the floor above 2% daylight factor)
Automated top and bottom vent to solar facade
Stack induced natural ventilation
Building-integrated photovoltaic array

Potential conflicts

In some instances the optimisation of the photovoltaic power generation runs counter to measures needed for low-energy design. The solar facade requires as much sunshine falling on it as possible, and, therefore, introduces the risk of overheating interior spaces; the materials of the facade are intrinsically low mass and are, therefore, incapable of providing thermal storage; the facade has relatively poor insulating properties and, therefore, is prone to heat loss; and its curtain wall construction inhibits the introduction of carefully graded, glare-free daylight into the building.

Where possible these apparent conflicts have been reconciled to be mutually reinforcing, and where this has not been possible a balance has been struck between respective requirements. Accordingly the heat from the facade (the conversion of sunlight into electricity in itself generates heat (see Chapter 2)) can be used in winter to assist in heating the building and in summer to pull air through the office space and out through the vents at the top of the facade. Lack of thermal mass is countered to some extent by specifying a concrete roof slab in place of the normal trussed and pitched roofs used elsewhere on the Park. The insulating properties of the solar facade are good in the context of glazing (U value: $1.2W/m^2K$ for the PV modules), but relatively poor compared to typical solid wall construction (U value: $0.4W/m^2K$). Heat loss, however, was minimised by ensuring that leakage of air through the building envelope as a whole is exceptionally low and by allowing heat to pass up the internal face of the facade.

The facade incorporates over 400,000 photovoltaic cells. The concentration of cell coverage was necessary to achieve the power output

Figure 10.6
View of interior

target. Bands of clear glazing have, however, been introduced into the facade to allow views out and ensure good internal light levels (see Figure 10.6). The balance between maximisation of power (from the opaque solar cells) and maximisation of daylight (a requirement of a daylight factor of at least 2% over 80% of the office floors) was arrived at by modelling glazing permutations using a 1:40 scale model under an artificial sky. The risk of glare is minimised by the introduction of semi-transparent modules (modules that have a lower cell count and are, therefore, able to let more daylight through) immediately above the clear glazed panels, and by provision for the introduction of locally controlled roller blinds capable of covering both the clear and semi-transparent modules.

Design for photovoltaics and for low-energy use have, therefore, to advance hand-in-hand; both are dependent on each other. The effective physical accommodation of each leads to conflicts which have to be resolved, and no two designers will resolve them in quite the same way. The Solar Office represents a particular balancing of these conflicts.

Natural ventilation and cooling

For the Solar Office, as typically for offices, winter heating is readily introduced. Here it is by some perimeter heating (plus potential heat reclaim from air at atrium roof level). The main issue is finding a passive approach to ventilation and to combating summer overheating.

The maximum width of floor to achieve single-sided ventilation (air in and out from the same window) is around 6–7m. With office-space floor widths for the Solar Office of 11–15m, cross-ventilation is needed if they are to be naturally ventilated.

Openable windows are readily introduced on the northerly facing facades. The design team did consider introducing openable windows in the PV facade, which is almost one-third clear glass, some of which could have had opening lights. But the difficulties of achieving weather-tightness on a 60° inclined facade, and the cost and complexity of providing mechanised window-opening, ruled it out.

Some other means, therefore, were needed to promote cross-ventilation within the office spaces. The two options for natural driving forces are the wind and stack effect. (Stack effect is the rising of currents of air that are warmer, thus less dense and more buoyant than surrounding air.) Both stack and wind are available here. Wind effects are typically several times more powerful than stack, especially for a relatively windy site such as this with a mean wind speed of 5–6m/s. The worst situation of hot still days is rare, but stack effect does increase as temperatures rise.

Stack effect is promoted by the PV facade itself. As the temperature rises at the back of the facade due to solar gain a current of warm air rises to roof level, helping to draw air out of the adjacent office spaces (see Figure 10.7). Mechanical vents have been installed at the bottom and top of the facade to help encourage this air flow, partly to keep the PV cooler. As the temperature of PV modules rise, their efficiency falls (see Appendix A).

Wind passing over a roof can create negative pressures (suction) so helping to draw air across the floors and up out of the building. There is also a danger that wind can blow in through the vents and reverse this air flow. Work by Tom Lawson at Bristol University has shown that by locating rooftop air outlets in a sheltered trough and including baffles at intervals to cope with winds blowing along the trough, it is possible to create at least some negative wind pressure in all conditions (see Figure 10.8).

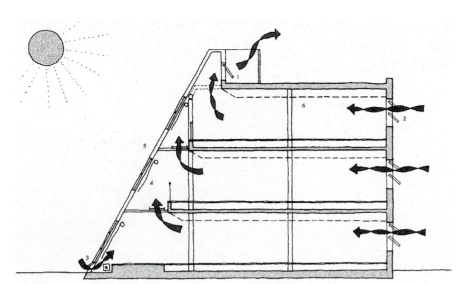

Figure 10.7
Sections: summer

PASSIVE SOLAR - SUMMERS DAY

Figure 10.8
Wind baffle and trough

For a naturally ventilated building, occupants are generally found to accept a wider variation in temperature than the standards typically set for air-conditioned buildings. Not having to raise or lower temperatures so much artificially to meet tighter standards also saves some energy. For the Solar Office, the summer maximum temperature standard is 26°C (dry resultant temperature). For design, internal heat loads were taken as:

- occupants $7W/m^2$
- lighting $15W/m^2$
- small power $25W/m^2$

Air-tightness of the building envelope also helps keep ventilation and heat losses under control. Part of the tender was to build in air-tightness and for that performance to be tested as part of handover. (A test standard of $10m^3/h/m^3$ at 50Pa was set. The Solar Office did better at 3.7.)

10.5 The PV facade

Integral design and installation

At its simplest, PV cells convert the sun's energy into DC electricity. The Solar Office has 352 modular panels each incorporating $100 \times 100mm$ cells. Almost all the facade is clad in one or two module arrangements, though there are a few specials, mainly to fit around the triangular main entrance.

Modules are wired down the mullions back to junction boxes and thence to inverters which convert DC electricity to AC. The junction boxes and the two smaller inverters are located in a trench at the foot of the facade; the two large inverters are under the staircases at the ends of the building.

As noted earlier, the PV installation is grid-connected. Compared with a self-contained installation this has several advantages:

- Reduced installation costs, particularly the cost of batteries.
- Ease of installation.
- Power when the PV supply is insufficient.
- Standard components.
- Reduction in complexity and maintenance.

The building's PV power output had to be quality-tested for constancy in voltage and frequency and acceptable variations in harmonic distortion before grid connection could be made.

PV facades as walls

The PV facade is basically a proprietary product, the Synergy Facade system from Schüco International. So the designers were not working out cladding from first principles. Their concerns were more about how a PV facade works as a wall in a low-energy building, for daylighting, thermally, in vent sealing and appearance (see Figure 10.9).

Figure 10.9
Section through facade

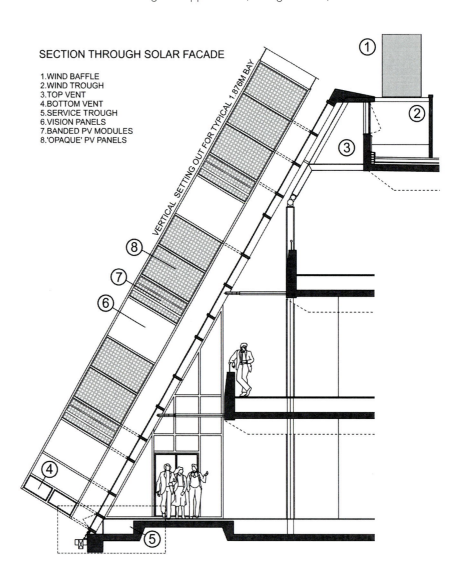

SECTION THROUGH SOLAR FACADE

1. WIND BAFFLE
2. WIND TROUGH
3. TOP VENT
4. BOTTOM VENT
5. SERVICE TROUGH
6. VISION PANELS
7. BANDED PV MODULES
8. 'OPAQUE' PV PANELS

VERTICAL SETTING OUT FOR TYPICAL 1.876M BAY

Daylighting

Most PV on buildings to date has been in small areas or spread on roofs or blank walls. But a whole building facade needs, among other things, to admit daylight and provide views out. The designers' response has been to make about 650m² of the 950m² facade PV with the rest clear glass. The PV cells are encapsulated in triple glazing. While some facade areas are densely packed with cells, in other areas cells are more spaced out to give a semi-transparent effect. These areas are located above the clear glass areas to reduce the contrast when looking out. Several configurations were modelled in an artificial sky.

Shading

Shading to limit overheating is normally most effective on the outside of a building. This works for windows but not for PV cells, which need maximum solar exposure. Shading to limit glare can just as well be on the inside of the glazing. The designers' preferred option here is motorised roller blinds inside the clear glazing areas.

Thermal performance

PV facades have limited thermal capacity – about which little can be done – and moderate insulation. The facade glazing build-up has a U-value of 1.2W/m²K, which is good for glazing but less impressive when compared to the masonry walls. The glazing build-up from the outside is:

- 5mm heat strengthened glass.
- 2mm cast resin encapsulating solar cells.
- 4mm heat strengthened glass (Parasol).
- 12mm krypton-filled void.
- 6mm laminated glass with low-E coating.

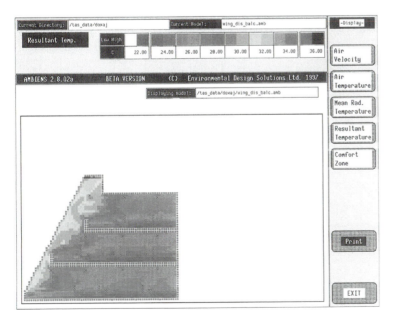

Figure 10.10
CFD plot

Figure 10.11
Day view

Figure 10.12 (right)
Night view

One option the designers considered was developing some form of cavity facade construction. This could have had the added benefit of improving PV efficiency. But there was no ready-made solution and not enough development time available. So instead they focused the CFD airflow modelling on refining the building section and improving dissipation of heat from the facade.

Vent sealing

A range of low-energy buildings have had problems getting motorised closers to close vents and windows tightly enough against their seals. This required extra care for the vents at the top and bottom of the PV facade (see Figure 10.9).

Appearance

With its reflective surface the PV facade changes appearance with the light. And with the clear glass bands there is a sense of transparency, particularly at night (see Figures 10.11 and 10.12). In selecting the PV cells, monocrystalline or polycrystalline cells were preferred to amorphous because of collection efficiency and durability. The vote went to polycrystalline, partly on the grounds of adding sparkle to the facade.

The mix of semi-transparent panels and clear glass can produce surprising and beautiful light effects inside (see Figure 10.13). The effect of the sun passing through the cells has been likened to a forest glade.

Figure 10.13
View from the interior

10.6   Implementation

PV procurement

PV on the scale of the Solar Office is innovative; the client was keen to minimise risk. Several steps helped:

- Choosing a tried-and-tested PV system.
- Letting the PV installation as a single package of supply, installation, interfacing and commissioning.
  This included Schüco bringing in a specialist electrical contractor from Germany with experience of PV.
- Given that the facade system provides sound cladding, in energy terms the PV is fail-safe. If it fails it generates nothing, the electricity bill goes up 25–30%, but occupants are not inconvenienced.

For the designers the tendering process was more difficult than usual. For other packages there was considerable reuse of methods and assemblies from previous buildings on the park. Aukett Associates had also developed various generic details. None of these fitted the PV package, which had to be tendered as a performance specification. There is as yet little in the way of standards or precedents to draw on, so the specifiers began largely from scratch. For example, discussions arose over:

- Tolerance on alignment of cells within a module.
- The acceptability of bubbles in the resin that encapsulates the cells.
- The appearance of circuit tape at module edges.
- A few cells that were torn during lamination (though testing showed no loss of performance).

There was also an initial difference between the 12-year warranty required by the developer and the 10 years customarily provided by the supplier.

It helps to be clear about what is meant when performance numbers are offered. PV installations are typically rated in kWp. That is 73.1kWp for the Solar Office. The "p" is for peak, and the "kWp" is the maximum output under standard radiation conditions (see Appendix A).

Less straightforward are efficiency ratings. Efficiencies for solar cells, like 14% for polycrystalline, are measures of the efficiency of converting solar radiation to electricity. But there is also system efficiency – the efficiency of converting solar radiation into electricity delivered from the system at the inverter. For the Solar Office that figure is calculated at 10.5%. Table 10.1 shows how Schüco arrived at this figure and thus where some of the losses are in the system.

Table 10.1
Predicted performance data

A. Incident radiation	
Solar radiation for the area (horizontal plane)	$950kWh/m^2/y$
Installation factor (inclination, orientation, coating)	$\times 1.04$
Adjusted solar radiation	$= 988kWh/m^2/y$
Active area of solar cells	$\times 532m^2$
Total radiation on facade	$= 525600kWh/y$
B. Element efficiencies	
Efficiency of solar cells (at 25°C)	$\times 0.14$
Reduction due to operating temperature	$\times 0.90$
Losses from cables	$\times 0.98$
Average efficiency of PV inverter	$\times 0.85$
C. Estimated annual energy output	$= 55200kWh/y$
D. System efficiency (estimated output/total radiation) 10.5%	

10.7 Performance

Maintenance

Maintenance of the facade is minimal; a wash down every six months externally and maybe once a year internally.

A cherry picker has been selected capable of reaching the inclined outer surface of the facade. It also folds compactly enough to enter and maintain the inner surface of the facade facing the atrium. For the office wings, the inside of the facade will be maintained using a proprietary ladder and plank system.

Selling the power to the grid

Although the UK has a non-fossil fuel obligation requiring electricity generating companies to become involved in selling electricity generated without fossil fuels, there was no specific requirement for them in 1998 to buy PV-generated electricity from grid-connected buildings. The project team found only one of the six regional generators ready to do so: Northern Electric.

Even then the standard contract started at 1MW and the annual administration charge was £1000 (later reduced to £500). Clearly some new thinking, and particularly regulation, is needed here.

10.8 Monitoring

Monitoring is covering the performance of the photovoltaic installation, energy consumption and internal comfort. This is being carried out over a two- to three-year period by Newcastle Photovoltaics Application Centre.

The PV system performance includes output measurement for all four sub-arrays as well as the complete system. Array temperatures are measured using embedded thermocouples in four of the modules, two on each side of the facade.

Energy consumption and internal comfort monitoring include measurements of the air temperature in the office space, atrium and the two passageways; humidity levels in the office space; electrical loads; gas usage; wind speed and direction. The activation of the automated solar facade vents and the upper window lights are recorded. This will allow the whole performance of the building to be assessed and the success of the design to be determined (see Figure 10.14).

Figure 10.14
Monitoring diagram

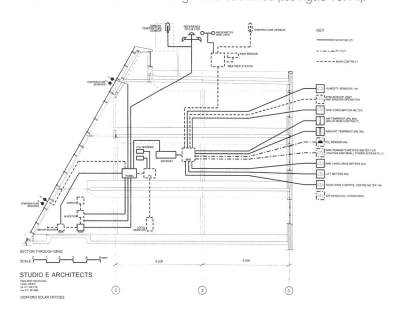

The results of the first year of running the PV installation have been published. After extrapolation for short periods of downtime the output matched predictions almost exactly (see Table 10.2). Results for the first two years will be available shortly. They confirm that output matches predictions.

Table 10.2
Performance data

Month	Monitoring fraction	Measured AC output (kWh)	Estimated loss due to inverter outage (kWh)	Estimated loss due to monitoring outage (kWh)	Corrected output (kWh)
Mar 1998	47	1530	0	1725	3225
Apr 1998	97	4607	0	142	4749
May 1998	85	5411	0	955	6366
June 1998	100	4240	927	0	5167
July 1998	100	4558	485	0	5043
Aug 1998	100	3277	1710	0	4987
Sept 1998	100	2740	497	0	3237
Oct 1999	100	3267	710	0	3977
Nov 1998	77	2330	0	695	3026
Dec 1998	—	—	0	1343	1343
Jan 1999	74	1987	0	698	2685
Feb 1999	100	3687	0	0	3687
All	0.89	37634	4329	5558	47492

Also, as part of the monitoring, a sophisticated touch-screen display has been set up in the atrium fed by the data loggers (see Figure 10.15).

Figure 10.15
Touch screen

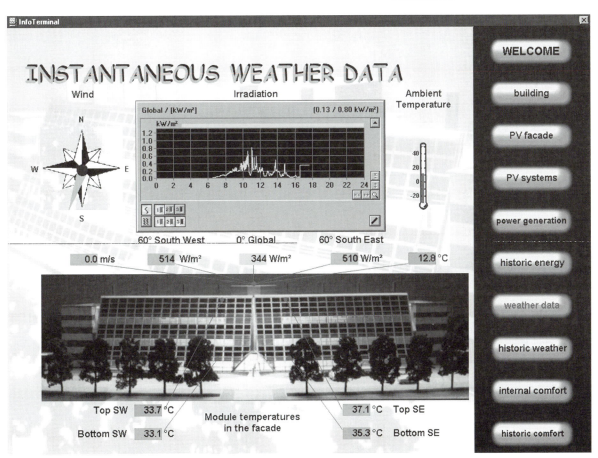

10.9 Program and budget

Informal discussions began in 1994 between Trevor Silver of Akeler and architect David Lloyd Jones of Studio E about the possibility of a low-energy design incorporating PV. At commercial rates of return PV does not currently pay for itself in fuel savings. So, as Doxford is in an appropriate development area, an application was made for funding support to the European Regional Development Fund (ERDF) to cover the major costs of the PV installation and some aspects of the proposed energy-efficiency measures.

A design team was formed during the latter half of 1996 and worked up the concept design far enough to describe the scheme to a range of potential funders.

ERDF support of £1.35m was agreed in December 1996. The client raised a further £2,875,000 in funding and the architects secured £111,000 from the Department of Trade and Industry towards design development, testing and monitoring. Full funding was secured early in 1997. A tight 15-month program was set for detailed design and construction. The start on site was 28 April 1997 with completion on 18 April 1998.

The degree of financial support needs setting in context. Excluding the other low-energy design support, the whole PV-related package cost around £950,000. Half of this is for the facade structure, the clear glazing, etc. The main PV installation of cells, wiring, inverters, etc., accounts for the other half (£470,000), or around £100/m^2 of the shell and core budget of £940/m^2. (Typically the fit-out budget would be another £100–200/m^2.)

Another perspective on this is that a typical all-in shell and core building in the area costs about £750/m^2. For a similar building planned for an adjacent plot on the park – without PV but with an enhanced passive low-energy specification – the architect calculates that the cost will be around £790/m^2.

With regard to the annual cost savings for the Solar Office, services engineers Rybka Battle have calculated an energy demand of 85kWh/m^2/y for a treated area of 4000m^2. Comparing this with a BRECSU Best Practice air-conditioned office produces the following annual savings:

- Reduced energy use from energy-saving measures £19,690.
- Reduced maintenance costs £32,000.
- Savings in grid-supplied electricity £3,320.

This gives a total estimated annual saving of £55,000 in running costs. (This assumes a cost of 2p/kWh for gas, 4p/kWh for electricity, but selling surplus electricity to the grid at 2p/kWh.)

10.10 Conclusion

The Solar Office represents the coming of age of building integrated photovoltaics. The building's ultimate success will be judged by the manner in which it meets the demands of the commercial marketplace. Previous projects have to a large extent been "demonstration" in purpose; future projects will increasingly incorporate photovoltaics on the basis of their proven value in contributing to environmentally sound energy strategies for buildings.

PROJECT PRINCIPALS

Client: Akeler PLC
Architect: Studio E Architects
Co-ordinating Architects: Aukett Associates
Structural Engineers: Whitby Bird and Partners
Building Services Engineers: Rybka Battle
Main Contractors: Bowmer and Kirkland
Solar facade: Schüco International
PV and building monitoring: Newcastle Photovoltaics Application Centre

11

The Earth Centre canopy

Peter Clegg

The Earth Centre was conceived as a visitor attraction providing both education and entertainment around environmental issues. It exists on a 300-acre site in one of the most environmentally devastated areas in the country: the coalfields of South Yorkshire. The masterplan for the Earth Centre (Figure 11.1) was to provide a large-scale visitor attraction providing new landscape for demonstrating the principles of ecological regeneration through a vibrant series of gardens, exhibitions which describe ecological problems and solutions, and architecture which demonstrates the potential of low-energy environmental design principles. Feilden Clegg Bradley Architects were appointed initially to help with the masterplan process, and thereafter as one of four architects working on the project were given the task of designing major buildings on the site.

Our brief was to design exhibition spaces, a cafeteria and shop as well as WCs and information point, all of which would provide the entrance to the Earth Centre site (Figure 11.2). Our strategy was to integrate a low-energy building with a highly visible solar generator which would be the first component in a strategy for the site to be self-sufficient in terms of power

Figure 11.1
Earth Centre masterplan with entrance building to the right

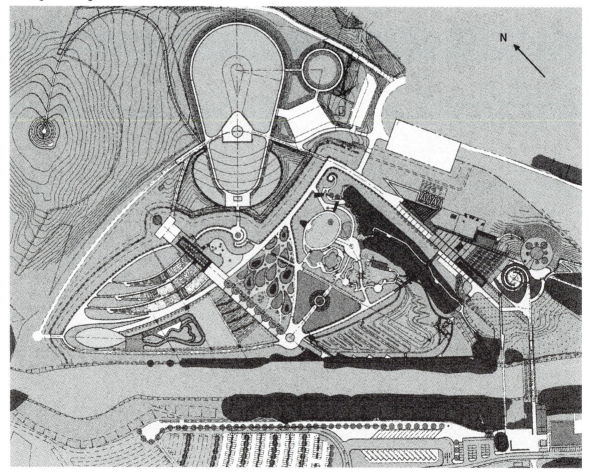

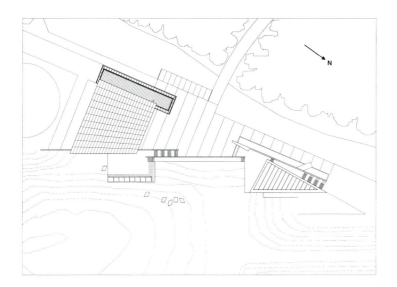

Figure 11.2 Entrance canopy
a) Plan

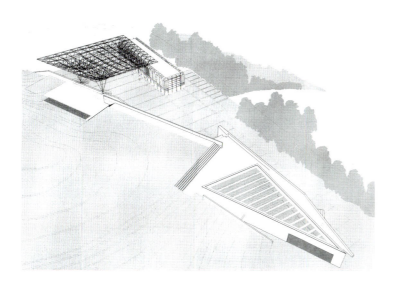

b) Aerial view from north-east

generation, the remainder ultimately to be provided by a wind generator located on an adjacent hillside and biomass fuel generated using material grown on site.

The buildings are located at the edge of a limestone escarpment, and a number of the major spaces, particularly those which do not require daylight such as the main exhibition hall, are buried in the existing hillside. The limestone of the escarpment, quarried less than half a mile away, forms the retaining wall to the new buried buildings. These buried structures, founded as they are on poor-quality ground, required very strong raft foundations. This led to the concept of a basement "labyrinth" which is used to store heat from internal gains in winter and benefits from night-time cooling in the summer. A building with extremely high internal heat gains therefore is able to operate without the use of air conditioning.

The bulk of the buildings are therefore built into the earth. One simple rectilinear building, however, floats free from the hillside and helps enclose a funnel-shaped arena which forms the entrance to the site. A canopy stretches across this trapezoidal-shaped space and shelters the ticket booths and main entrance area. The canopy designed with Atelier One Structural Engineers is a distorted timber space frame (Figure 11.3) constructed using roundwood poles of indigenous softwood with galvanised steel connectors.

Figure 11.3
View from approach

The elaborate geometry created by the trapezoidal frame and the almost random supporting posts forms a dynamic contrast with the purity and simplicity of the adjacent building forms.

The canopy is roofed with photovoltaic cells embedded in glass. The cells are spaced 4mm apart with a 60mm space round the edge so that approximately 25% of the daylight striking the canopy will penetrate through it. This dappled light will provide some welcome shading in midsummer, and the semi-transparency, combined with the complex geometry of the timber structure, will create an abstract representation of a living forest: processed timber forms the trunks and branches of the "trees" with photovoltaic cells capturing and transforming sunlight as do the leaves of a tree.

Studies were carried out looking at various configurations for the arrays of cells. "Ridge and furrow" type solutions, whilst benefiting from increased isolation due to the steeper angle, also meant a reduced collector area and a more complex structural arrangement of guttering, etc. The individual arrays would have to be spaced further apart, particularly at more optimum and steeper collector angles in order to avoid overshading in winter. In the end the configuration chosen was to provide a flat plate to the entire roof sloping at an angle of 5° towards the south (Figure 11.4). Water collects at the front edge of the canopy in a single large gutter (Figure 11.5) which also acts as a wind deflector, and the water is discharged into a holding tank in the earth bank at the side of the buried buildings.

The installation is of monocrystalline silicon cells with a minimum collection efficiency of 15.5% set between 2 panes of glass. Each panel is $3.0 \times 1.2m$ in area, using cells by BP Solar, manufactured by Pilkington Solar International in Germany, and supported by a Schüco aluminium glazing system.

The output of the 1000m² of collector array is just over 107kW peak yielding a total potential of 77,000kWh of generated electricity per year.

Figure 11.4
Sections through the canopy

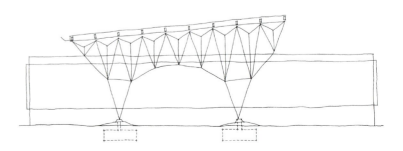

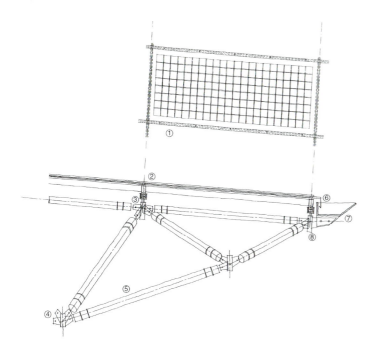

Figure 11.5
Section at south edge gutter

Key
1 Aluminium pressure plate to long edges
2 Clear silicone sealant joint
3 Extruded aluminium framing used as cable trunking
4 Fabricated galvanised mild steel connector
5 Rounded softwood struts
6 Anodized aluminium flashing
7 Galvanised mild steel gutter
8 Modified space frame connector with gutter support bracket

This will provide approximately 20% of the annual electrical consumption of the entrance buildings.

The majority of the panels will be connected to a single central inverter designed and installed by Ecofys from Holland, with DC cabling running immediately beneath the collectors. For experimental purposes, however, 22 of the modules will incorporate mini-inverters bonded to the underside of the panel so that the output of the panel itself will be AC electricity.

The instances when there is an oversupply of electricity from the generator are very infrequent. Currently negotiations are still underway with Yorkshire Electricity, the supply authority, which will determine whether it is worth while overcoming the safety and technical problems associated with grid connection, or whether it is simpler to forego collection at times when the solar electricity is not usable on site. Particular problems associated with the grid in the area, combined with what would seem to be excessive metering costs irrespective of the quantity of electricity sold back to the grid, currently mitigate against the installation of a grid connection.

The scheme will be installed with the benefit of a THERMIE grant from the European Union as well as monies from the Millennium Commission and the European Regional Development Fund. The intention is that the collector should make a significant statement at the main entrance of the Earth Centre emphasising the importance of on-site electricity generation using photovoltaics as a way of reducing dependency on fossil fuels and therefore reducing greenhouse gas emissions. Construction commenced on site in December 1999 and completion is scheduled for sometime in late 2001.

Canopy structures such as the Earth Centre could provide appropriate locations for photovoltaic installations without the complexities of having PVs integrated into the building skin. Shelter structures such as the Jourda and Perraudin enclosure for the Government Training Centre at Herne-Sodingen in Germany illustrate ways in which an umbrella of semi-transparent glass/glass photovoltaics can provide a shaded and sheltered inside/outside space for a whole group of buildings which could then be constructed to a lower standard of weathertightness. Canopy structures could be useful in a wide range of situations from transport interchanges (bus and train stations) to shopping malls, sheltered streets (as appropriate in hot climates for providing solar shading as in temperate climates for providing rain shelter) and outdoor arenas and stadia.

If PVs become cost-effective in their own right, we will undoubtedly see their use spreading beyond building integration. Harvesting solar energy could become an alternative agricultural process with PVs covering areas of open countryside to replace declining agricultural crops or bio-mass cultivation, but they would be more appropriately incorporated into urban areas over large-scale industrial buildings, car parks or even over structures for roads and railways where they could also provide some acoustic baffling. The concept of the sheltered or partially shaded street, using glass/glass PVs to help create a more appropriate external micro-climate, is one of the more exciting and, as yet, unexplored uses of the new technology. Small-scale, building-integrated systems are less likely to be cost-effective and could tend to compete with windows and rooflights to the detriment of natural daylighting and ventilation. The impact of photovoltaics on urban design as well as architecture needs imaginative exploration.

PROJECT PRINCIPALS

Client:	The Earth Centre
Architect:	Feilden Clegg Bradley Architects: Mike Keys, Peter Clegg
Structural Engineers:	Atelier One, Carpenter Oak
Project and Construction Managers:	Taylor Woodrow

12

University of Cambridge, Department of Earth Sciences, BP Institute

Chris Cowper and Philip Armitage

12.1   Introduction

The BP Institute is a major new research initiative at Cambridge University funded by BP AMOCO and involving five departments: Earth Sciences (which will provide the administration), Applied Mathematics, Chemistry, Chemical Engineering, and Engineering. The Institute will consist of a University Officer from each Department; a Professor, who will be the first Director, and four Lecturers, whose posts will be endowed by BP AMOCO. The officers will hold their posts in the relevant departments, where they will do their teaching. Their research groups will, however, be housed within the Institute at the Department of Earth Sciences

Since the University Officers will hold their appointments in one of the Departments involved, rather than in the Institute, it was felt to be particularly important for the long-term health of the Institute that it should provide a congenial working environment, and that it should be thoroughly integrated into the existing community of scientists at the Department of Earth Sciences. These concerns have governed its size, location and design.

BP AMOCO has a long-standing interest in energy production and was very keen to incorporate PV power generation in this new research facility. However, this interest only became apparent after the overall location and form of the building had been determined. This project therefore illustrates the incorporation of a PV installation into a building which had not been specifically designed for it, and the issues addressed here have broad application to large numbers of existing buildings.

12.2   Site

The site for the new building lies within the mature gardens of Madingley Rise (see Figure 12.1), a large Victorian house occupied by the Department of Earth Sciences, and describes an arc between the house to the south and its stables building to the north. It will provide 816m^2 of accommodation, arranged on three floors, comprising a full ground and first with a basement floor on the western side only, and will accommodate 30 people. Discussions with the Department indicated that the best way to suit the needs of the research staff would be to provide a number of individual offices of varying size, as well as an area in open plan format, together with a director's office, meeting room, and ancillary service areas. Access to the completed building will be from the existing roads currently serving both Earth Sciences and the Institute of Astronomy.

12.3   Brief

The brief for the new building was unusual in the degree of involvement by both the Department of Earth Sciences and BP AMOCO. Apart from the

Figure 12.1
Photograph of site and existing
buildings

specification of both the type and the extent of the accommodation required, detailed discussions were held with all interested members of the Department during the design process. A number of key objectives were identified as follows:

1.   It was noted by the Department that the house, which was constructed of brickwork walls, a tiled roof, and wooden painted windows, had lasted extremely well and remained robust and surprisingly adaptable – arguably, it was observed, rather longer than buildings for other Departments constructed in the last 30 to 40 years.
2.   The new building should be at least as easy to maintain as the existing, and eschew design complexity which might lead to problems in the future.
3.   The new BP Institute should respect the existing Victorian house in terms of proportion and materials and should have a contemporary design commensurate with the image of the company.
4.   Issues relating to energy use and conservation were identified as of paramount importance, especially in view of the business of BP AMOCO. The company put forward the use of PV panels during the design, for practical use and as a showcase for BP Solar.
5.   Finally the identity of both the existing Department of Earth Sciences and BP AMOCO should be separately identifiable and maintained, whilst at the same time combining the two organisations together to allow maximum collective use of information and research.

12.4   Site planning issues

The approach to the Department of Earth Sciences immediately creates a dilemma, in that the existing house is clearly visible, but, in turn, entirely hides from view the site for the new Institute (see Figure 12.2). In addition, separate entrances are required to the existing Department in Madingley Rise and the new building in order that the individual identities and independence of the two are maintained. Since the objective is to give equal weight to both, the site plan strategy gives a greater visual weight to the existing house (and Department), but at the same time identifies the entrance and presence of the new Institute.

The entrance canopy is a contemporary reinterpretation in glass and stainless steel of the existing loggia or covered entrance to the Department's

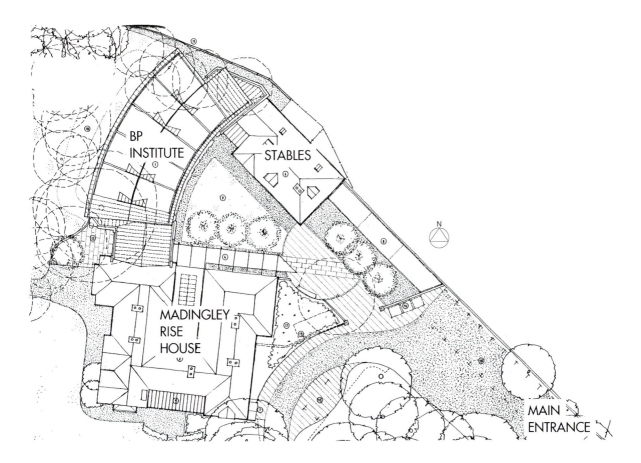

BP
INSTITUTE

STABLES

N

MADINGLEY
RISE
HOUSE

MAIN
ENTRANCE

Figure 12.2
Site plan

main entrance on the south side and leads the visitor directly into the entrance foyer of the new building. This space will be the route from one building to the other and will also perform the function of reception. New doors between the new entrance hall and the existing tea room allow the two spaces to be used together for larger functions. The existing lightwell in the centre of the old house has a new glazed roof and forms an extension to the tea room. This is seen as the most important space in the Department, providing an area to meet and talk through work and ideas, as well as providing a small informal lecture room.

Great care has been taken to ensure that the different scales and characters of Madingley Rise, the existing stables buildings and the new building constructed between them are properly reconciled. The elevation to the west, facing the gardens, is constructed predominantly of brick as a series of interlayered planes echoing the composition of the original house elevations. The asymmetric arrangement of the fenestration on this side complements the old house and contrasts with the more structured full-height bays facing the courtyard to the east. These elements are designed as four full-height bays with aluminium window systems. The roof of the building will be finished with terned stainless steel, which has a finish similar to weathered lead, with raised sections of the roof plane finished in natural slate to provide a texture similar to the roof of Madingley Rise.

12.5 Photovoltaics and energy strategy

The energy efficiency, maintenance and use of the building were constant themes running throughout the design. In order to meet the client's objectives, simple and robust strategies have been adopted wherever possible. The design team is working with BP Solar who will provide the PV installation (modules, wiring and power conditioning equipment) as a turnkey package, to be installed during the final stages of the main building contract.

The use of the PV panels has necessitated decisions on the form and construction of the building envelope. The main part of the BP Institute is curved in plan to link the existing buildings and has a pitched roof – the radius of curvature at the ridge line is 28m and occupies 46° of arc in plan (see Figure 12.3). The principal facades and roof planes face approximately east–west and there are no significant, unshaded south-facing surfaces. The east–west orientation of the new building, with the south side obscured by the existing Department, immediately presents a problem for the use of PVs. Panels mounted within the roof plane were not an option due to the east–west aspect of the roof. The design approach adopted offers a solution to a common problem by the use of south-facing free-standing angled glass panels which form a series of outstretched wings arrayed along the ridge of the main roof (see Figure 12.4). This is made possible by the division of the roof into a series of slated segments, with channels between them, finished in terned stainless steel. This segmental division of the roof covering both contributes to the design concept, and provides for the proper weathered construction of the steel mounting arms for the panels, and for their subsequent maintenance and cleaning. Access is gained to each panel from fixed ladders at either end of the ridge, which is designed as a small walkway. A continuous rail runs along the ridge for the attachment of safety harnesses to allow maintenance crews to walk down each segmental division to access the panels.

Figure 12.3
Roof plan

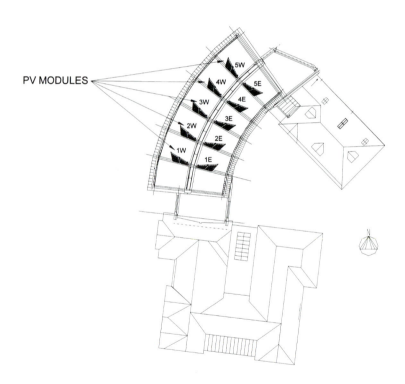

Figure 12.4
Garden (west) elevation

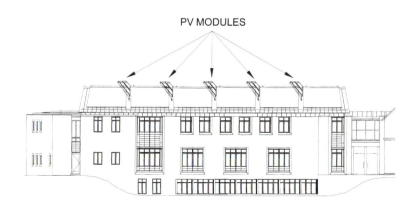

Figure 12.5
Layout and details of PV modules

STEEL MAST

PV MODULE

CANTILEVER BRACKET

ROOF PENETRATION

BRACKET SOCKET WELDED TO TRUSS

The panels are constructed using the "Planar" glazing system manufactured by Pilkington (see Figure 12.5). The glass is fixed back, using "Planar" fixing bolts to 76mm diameter steel masts. The panel itself is a sandwich comprising a 15mm clear toughened glass base, a 2mm layer of monocrystalline PV cells embedded in resin, and a top layer of 6mm low-iron glass. Wiring will be taken from junction boxes located on either side of the central supports via grommeted holes into the roof void where the power conditioning equipment will be housed. The panel and support construction has been designed to be as visually light as possible while resisting design wind loadings of approximately 1900Pa. This design solution has the advantage of providing excellent ventilation around the panels, minimising the reduction in PV output due to overheating.

The aggregate area of panels was initially chosen to offset 5% of the estimated electricity consumption of the building, a value which was arrived at as being the maximum achievable contribution within the confines of the existing building design. The electrical consumption of the BP Institute is estimated at 55MWh/y (95kWh/m^2/y), resulting in a target output of 2.75MWh/y. Since a typical monocrystalline PV installation produces approximately 100kWh/m^2/y, the necessary panel area was estimated at 27.5m^2. The overall appearance of the panels was determined aesthetically and their final shape and orientation have been arrived at by a careful balancing of several conflicting factors:

• The maximum panel dimensions are limited to approximately 2000mm × 1500mm for both structural and fabrication reasons; the PV cells are arrayed at fixed centres of 127mm.
• The need to keep the top of each trapezoidal panel horizontal while tilted at an angle to improve efficiency and allowing a regular feathering of PV cells.
• Cost.

The total active panel area achieved in practice is 24.8m^2, which is 10% less than the target area – caused mainly by the need to further divide each panel into two to incorporate a central support.

PV-generated power will be used within the building by being supplied to the general power installation via power-conditioning equipment to produce 240V AC synchronised with the mains (see Figure 12.6). It is connected to the national grid via the electrical installation. Negotiations with the

Figure 12.6
PV installation schematic

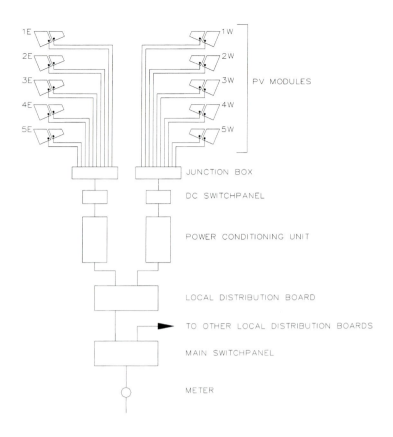

electricity supply utility are still at an early stage, but initial indications are that simple one-way metering will be appropriate since almost all the generated power will be used within the building under normal operating conditions. The PV installation is required to comply with Engineering Recommendation G77 produced by the Electricity Association, which specifies the requirements for small grid-connected electricity generating installations.

There are a number of issues which will need to be addressed during the design of the electrical side of the PV installation in conjunction with BP AMOCO. Each panel faces in a different direction on plan, resulting in different annual efficiencies (see Figure 12.7), instantaneous outputs (see Figure 12.8) and different maximum power points (MPP). There is an

Figure 12.7
PV module annual efficiencies

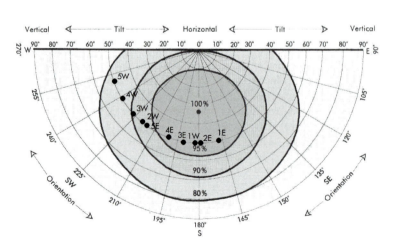

100% corresponds to the tilt and orientation which
gives the maximum total annual solar radiation
(1093kWh/m²/y on a surface oriented due south at a tilt of 32°)
on a fixed surface in Cambridge (52°13' N, 0°06'W)

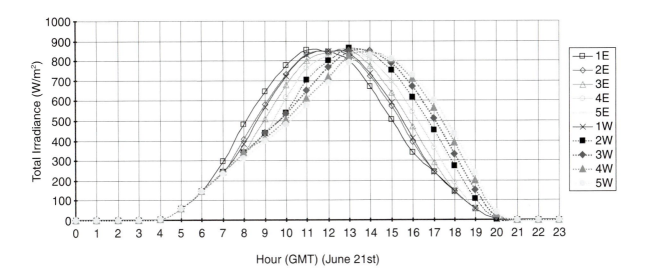

Hour (GMT) (June 21st)

optimum number of power-conditioning units, which balances the efficiency of the installation (ie matching the MPPs of all the modules as closely as possible) against cost since the relative costs of the power-conditioning equipment reduce with increasing nominal power rating. Also the ridge causes partial shading of the modules at either end of the day. Differential shading of individual cells in a string affects the output of the entire string, and therefore the wiring of the strings of cells within each panel will need to be carefully configured in order to minimise the reduction of module output under these conditions. The details of these aspects have yet to be resolved.

PV-generated electricity is only part of the energy strategy of the project. As part of a life cycle cost analysis we investigated optimum insulation thicknesses. The lifetime for the study was defined as 25 years by the University. Particular attention was paid to optimising the insulation levels to achieve the lowest total cost of installed insulation and fuel use for this lifetime. A set of thermal models of the building was constructed which allows for the effects of site geography, heating plant operation, incidental heat gains, thermal mass, solar gains, ventilation and infiltration. Each model incorporated different fabric insulation levels. The annual energy use was calculated by determining the heat flow for each hour of a statistically average year. Fuel costs were calculated from the predicted energy use for the lifetime. Not surprisingly, we did not find any projections of fuel costs for the next 25 years and the calculations therefore use today's costs only. Installed rates for differing thicknesses of insulation are readily available. Finally, the sum of lifetime fuel and insulation costs were plotted against U-value, and the U-value representing minimum total cost established. The optimal overall U-value for the BP Institute is 0.23W/m²K. We have achieved an overall U-value of 0.24W/m²K by using 85mm mineral wool batts in the external walls (U-value = 0.35W/m²K) and 400mm mineral wool blanket in the roof (U-value = 0.085W/m²K). All windows are double glazed units with low emissivity coatings.

The existing house and stables were heated by a single oil-fired boiler. In order to increase annual efficiency and reduce pollution, the existing oil-fired heating plant is being replaced by four modular condensing gas-fired boilers which will serve both the existing buildings and the BP Institute. The boilers have ultra-low NO$_x$ burners and are controlled to maximise condensation (efficiency) during operation.

Figure 12.8
PV module instantaneous irradiances (midsummer day)

It was agreed with both the users and the client at an early stage that the offices would be naturally ventilated, with a strategy targeted to ensure that peak internal temperatures were no more than 3°C above external ambient temperatures. Thermal modelling of a typical room showed that it was important to minimise the need for artificial lighting, provide solar shading, and that night-time ventilation coupled with adequate thermal mass would be necessary. The shallow plan of the offices (4.5m) allows simple single-sided ventilation. It was essential that the provision of night-time ventilation did not compromise the primary security of the building as it will contain large numbers of computers.

A strategy was devised whereby ventilation was provided via vertical panels adjacent to each window comprising an outer weather and security louvre and an inner, manually operated, centre pivoted, insulated panel (see Figure 12.9). The construction types proposed (concrete floors with carpet tiles, plastered masonry external walls, plasterboard studwork internal partitions and plasterboard suspended ceilings), and the predicted internal and solar heat gains, dictated an average night-time ventilation rate of 3ac/h. The height and free area of the panels allow this night-time ventilation rate to be provided by stack effect only since wind speeds tend to be lowest during the night.

Unfortunately the proposals for the ventilation panels came at the same time as the introduction of additional accommodation in the form of the basement, and ultimately have not been incorporated for cost reasons. Daytime ventilation is provided by casement opening windows, and secure night-time ventilation is allowed for by security restraints on these. If windows are not left open at night peak daytime temperatures are expected to exceed the design goal by up to 2°C.

The glazed areas of the windows were sized to provide an average daylight factor of 2.5%. More than half the plan area of each room (see Figure 12.10) has a daylight factor of greater than 3%, which allows these spaces to be used for an average of 85% of normal working hours without supplementary artificial lighting. Ideally the artificial lighting would be automatically controlled in response to daylight level and occupant presence. The client was wary of the long-term reliability of these systems

Figure 12.9
Detail of ventilation panel

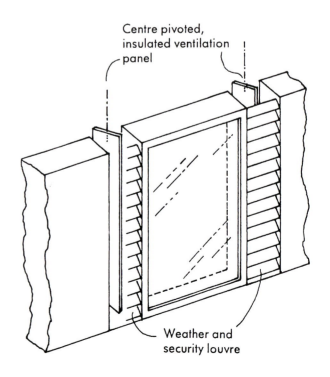

Centre pivoted,
insulated ventilation
panel

Weather and
security louvre

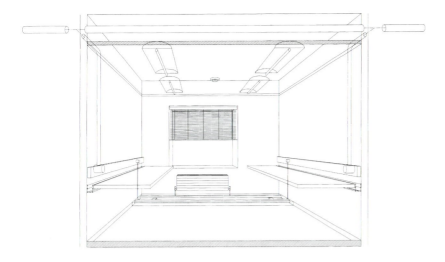

Figure 12.10
Typical room.

Width = 4.5m
Depth = 4.0m
Window area = 1.7sq.m

and internal lighting is manually switched. All office lighting is from fluorescent lamps with high-frequency control gear, and is zoned into perimeter and inner switch groups.

The site is well planted with existing deciduous trees on the west side and planting is proposed for the east side, permitting solar control to be limited to internal venetian blinds. Interpane venetian micro-blinds were suggested to allow window operation to be unaffected by blind position, but were ultimately rejected as a result of both maintenance concerns and visual intrusion.

12.6   Conclusion

This project demonstrates that it is possible to successfully integrate PV electricity generation into a building that has not been specifically planned for it, and which at first sight seems almost entirely unsuitable. Considerable effort has been expended to arrive at an appropriate design to complement the architecture, and to understand the particular aspects of this installation which may affect its overall performance.

Construction was completed in late 2000. The building is currently being monitored during its first year of operation to obtain feedback on the actual versus predicted performance.

PROJECT PRINCIPALS

Client:	University of Cambridge
Architect:	Cowper Griffith Associates
Services Consultant:	Max Fordham & Partners
Structural Engineer:	Hannah Reed Associates
Quantity Surveyor:	Sherriff Tiplady Associates

13

Haileybury Imperial College

Bill Watts

13.1   Introduction

Haileybury Imperial College is a private school in the green belt north of London. In autumn 1997 the school commissioned Studio E Architects to design and obtain planning permission for two boarding houses for girls. Situated on a relatively tight site around a pond at the bottom of the headmaster's garden, both houses contain dormitory and study bedroom accommodation for 66 girls and residential facilities for both the staff and the house mistress. Figure 13.1 shows an aerial view of the school.

Having gained permission on this sensitive site, the school built the first boarding house which was occupied in autumn 1999. Based on its success, the school commissioned the second house for completion in autumn 2001.

As a parallel exercise the design team was funded by the DTI (via an ETSU grant) to investigate the issues surrounding installing building-integrated PVs (BIPV) on the second house. The attraction being that, if built, the two

Figure 13.1
Haileybury Imperial College: aerial view

buildings with identical briefs and occupancy could be compared in capital-construction and energy-running costs.

13.2 Design considerations

The school did not intend to occupy the building outside school term time. This, in conjunction with the fact that the building was largely empty during the day as the pupils were in classes, meant that the electricity generated by the PV array during the day and in the summer did not match the building load. However, the PV electricity could be readily used elsewhere on the large school campus when available.

The buildings on the campus are fed by a number of separately metered supplies from several South East Electricity Board (SEEB) owned transformers. The first girls' boarding house had a new small (72kVA) transformer and metered supply intended to serve both it and the subsequent Phase II house. Therefore the simplest way of transferring electricity from the BIPV boarding house to the rest of the campus was via the SEEB low-voltage and high-voltage network (see Figure 13.2) . The alternative of running a separate LV cable around the site would have been very expensive.

Negotiations with SEEB were very encouraging. In their role as network providers and electricity suppliers they offered to credit any electricity exported by the PVs against the electricity used by other buildings on the campus at any one time. This effectively meant that the value of the PV electricity to the school was always the on-peak rate it was paying to the utility. The basis for this offer was:

1.   The electricity produced by the PVs would be small compared to the consumption of the campus, so it would not be exported outside the campus.

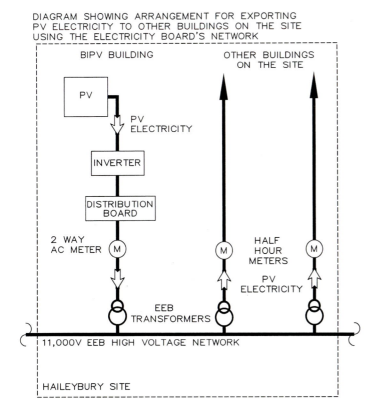

DIAGRAM SHOWING ARRANGEMENT FOR EXPORTING PV ELECTRICITY TO OTHER BUILDINGS ON THE SITE USING THE ELECTRICITY BOARD'S NETWORK

Figure 13.2
Arrangement for exporting PV electricity to other buildings on the site using the SEEB's network

2.   To credit the electricity produced against that used elsewhere, the PV building had to have an import/export meter. Other meters on the site would need to be of the type that communicated back to a central sorting system that monitors half hourly electricity consumption in real time from each consumer.

3.   The central sorting system would aggregate the net electricity consumption of all the meters on the site on a half hourly basis and the school would pay only for the imported electricity.

SEEB said that there would be a charge for setting this arrangement up and that they would expect to have a contract to supply the college with electricity over the next three years.

Without the constraint of matching the PV output to the needs of the building, the study looked at various massing arrangements, shown in Figure 13.3, to see what would provide the greatest area of PV. This resulted in a range of arrays of between 450m^2 and 1100m^2.

Figure 13.3
Option diagrams

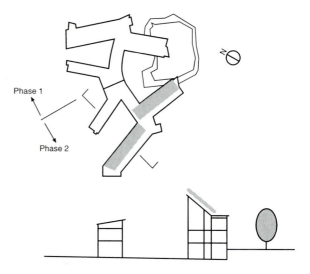

1. Application of PVs to south-facing roofs of the conventional Phase II building. PV area 500m^2.

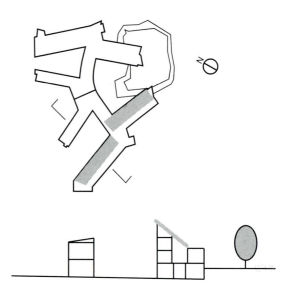

2. A rearrangement of the Phase II plan to provide a more compact footprint and with the introduction of a fourth floor and linear atrium space. The PVs are disposed on a single inclined south-facing roof. PV area 450m^2.

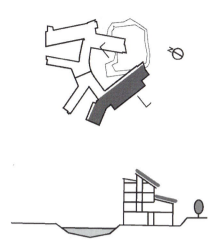

2a. Similar to Option 2 but with the elimination of the linear atrium and the stepping down of the section to the south to provide two inclined south-facing roofs. PV area 500m^2.

3. The accommodation deployed behind a continuous inclined facade. PV area 1100m^2.

4. The accommodation deployed on a tower. PV area 700m^2.

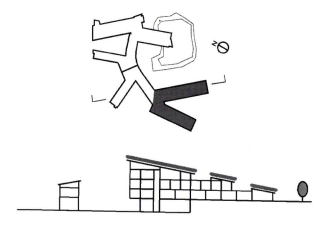

5. The accommodation deployed in a V-shaped building with the two wings reducing in height along their length and the PV array stepping down each wing. PV area 765m^2.

The planning constraint of the conventional scheme insisted, amongst other things, that the roof line was kept below an existing adjacent building and that the large trees were kept. It was decided to take a scheme forward to the planners that was one floor taller than the conventional scheme and that involved cutting down some tall trees. This change of massing made the building less expensive to construct as the footprint and retaining ground structures were reduced, which released money for the PV installation.

Figure 13.4
The design strategy of Option 2a
(Figure 13.3) after further development

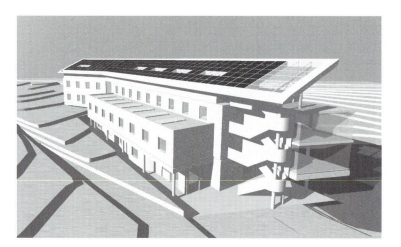

The more compact form also had a lower fabric heat loss; the potential PV area was 500m^2.

A Framework 5 application to the EU for financial support for the scheme was submitted in the summer of 1999. While the EU grant application was being processed, the design of the "conventional" Phase II building was progressing to meet the school's program to start on site in April 2000.

By the time confirmation of the EU grant had been finalised, the "conventional" design had been completed. To save redesign fees needed to develop the preferred PV option, it was decided to adapt the "conventional" Phase II scheme to accommodate PVs. This was not too dissimilar to Option 1. The size of the array was reduced to 250m^2 to match the funding (see Note 1).

On the basis of being "green" in energy terms the building did get planning consent. However, the planners reserved judgement on the felling of the tall trees until the actual reduction in output caused by them was demonstrated (see Figure 13.5).

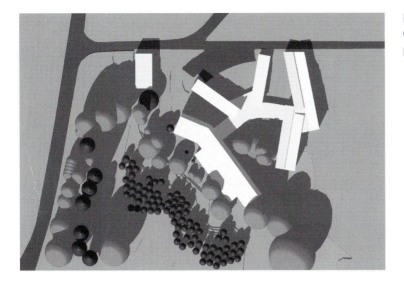

Figure 13.5
Over-shading of the site with trees in place

13.3 Heat recovery

The use of the heat from the back of the PVs was considered. It was clear that most of the energy and heat was collected over the summer when the hot water/heating load was light – especially given that the school was empty through the holidays. It was decided to look at seasonally storing the thermal energy from the PVs in the ground. To do this heat needed to be collected by a fluid medium so it could be transported into the ground.

Shell Solar, in connection with the Dutch Research Organisation ECN, were developing a PV and thermal solar hybrid panel. This comprises a monocrystalline PV panel bonded to a liquid thermal collector, with a glazed cover to reduce heat loss. Conversations with Shell Solar suggested that the loss of electrical output, due to the glazing removing some of the light, could be regained if the cooling medium was kept to 35°C to cool the panel. Losses of 10% over a "standard" air-cooled BIPV module could be expected with water at 55°C (see Figure 13.6).

Figure 13.6
PV and thermal solar hybrid panel

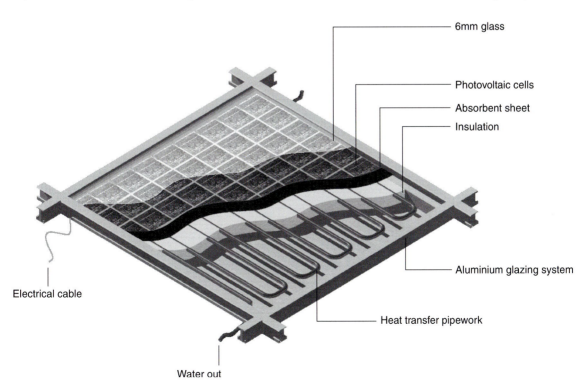

6mm glass

Photovoltaic cells

Absorbent sheet

Insulation

Aluminium glazing system

Heat transfer pipework

Electrical cable

Water out

The ground is dense saturated London clay. The ground's impermeability means that the heat stored would not be carried away by water flow. However, there is a heat loss due to conduction that is minimised by decreasing the surface area to volume ratio. The initial proposal was to use the ground below the building as a heat store by using the structural piles as heat exchangers. Polythene pipes cast into the concrete of the piles would carry the heating fluid from the solar panels to transfer the heat into the ground. However, concerns about the thermal expansion of the piles and the clay causing excessive movement meant that this idea was dropped.

Phase change materials were examined as an alternative to the ground as a store. Such materials require a great deal of heat to change state from solid to liquid or liquid to gas and the process occurs at a constant temperature. Changing from solid to liquid does not involve a great change of volume, which makes it ideal for heat storage. However, a material such as water which freezes at 0°C is not very useful for storing heat needed to warm a building. Alternative materials that change at other temperatures are commercially available, but providing an adequate quantity of these for the scheme was costed at about £500,000. This was more than the budget would allow and so this option was rejected.

The scheme is being developed with a separate ground heat store remote from the building. Ways of dropping small pipes into the ground are being investigated. The stiffness of the clay makes simply driving the pipes in difficult, so boring 150–250mm diameter boreholes and dropping the pipes in is under review.

The current design employs a plan area of 15m × 15m and is about 30m in depth. The volume of about 6750m^3 is intended to store 82,000kWh annually with a 15°C temperature swing in the clay. Using guidelines from Sweden we estimate that over the year 50% of the heat will be lost through conduction at the temperatures we are intending to use.

Swedish work[1] on the conductivity and diffusivity of the clay suggested that we needed 2m spacings between the boreholes.

The lower the temperature at which the heat is collected and stored, the better. Lower solar panel temperatures increase the PV electrical output. Being cooler also increases the net amount of solar heat collected as the heat lost from the panel to the surrounding air is reduced. Similarly, the heat loss from the thermal ground store is a function of how hot it is.

It was decided to use the heat from the store and panels to warm the incoming outside air, rather than heat the spaces directly (see Figure 13.7). The external air temperatures during the heating season are lower than the internal space temperature (obviously). This being the case, heat at or below room temperature can provide useful heat into the air. The ventilation scheme comprises an air handling unit with two heater batteries. The heat transfer fluid circulating through the thermal panels on the roof could be directly connected to the first heater battery. With the external air at 0°C, any solar gain will be collected in the thermal panels increasing the fluid temperature to 8°C on a sunny day. This fluid will heat the incoming air from 0 to 5°C. The second heater battery connects to the ground store which will heat the air further. Again with this method it is possible to extract useful heat from the ground at below room temperature.

The temperatures of the heat store, solar panels and outside air systems are dynamic and vary throughout the year. The thermal ground store will be divided into two zones: a core and a perimeter. The two zones will be used to take full advantage of temperature gradients in the various systems. The central zone will be "hot" and the outer one "warm". With maximum summer insolation, hot water at 52°C from the panels is first passed through

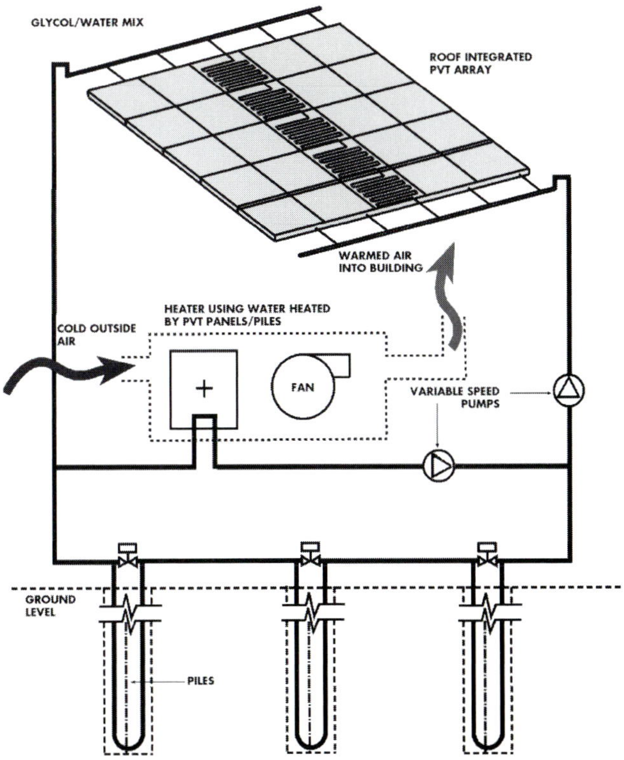

Figure 13.7
Energy system

the inner core giving up half its heat before going through the outer piles at 42°C and finally returning to panels at 32°C. The inner core warms to 35°C and the outer to 25°C. Through the year heat will be lost from the store but this is minimised by reducing the size of the high temperature part. At the beginning of the heat season, the temperature in the outer layer may be enough to heat the supply air. During the coldest part of the year, both zones will be used.

In the spring the temperature of the outer zone is too low to heat the warmer external air and the heat remaining in the inner core is used.

The pipework to the piles is arranged so the heat flow can be managed in this way.

13.4 Conclusion

Initial studies suggest that the 250m^2 of panels will annually collect about 110,000kWh of heat and 25,000kWh of electricity. Of the 110,000kWh, 30,000kWh will be collected during the heating season and used directly. 80,000kWh will be collected through the summer and stored. Of this 80,000kWh, it is estimated that 40,000kWh will be lost, leaving 40,000kWh of available heat. The project will provide useful data to validate these predictions.

REFERENCE

1. Göran Hellström, (1991), Ground Heat Storage Thermal Analyses of Duct Storage Systems. Department of Mathematical Physics, University of Lund, Sweden.

PROJECT PRINCIPALS

Client:	Haileybury and Imperial Services College
Architect:	Studio E Architects
Services Engineer:	Max Fordham & Partners
Structural Engineer:	Dewhurst MacFarlane
Landscape Architect:	PTP Landscape & Urban Design
Quantity Surveyor:	The Spicer Partnership
PV Consultant:	Shell Solar
PV Thermal Panel Research Consultant:	Netherlands Energy Research Foundation
Environmental Systems Consultant:	Esbensen Consulting Engineers

NOTE

At the time of going to press the client had decided to proceed with the conventional version of the Phase II building without PVs, due to the uncertainties in the procurement program in the PV version. It is hoped that the funding and research can be transferred to another project.

14

PVs in perspective

Bill Dunster

14.1   A mission for the new millennium

A decade of environmental research on a series of projects ranging from the New Parliamentary Building at Westminster (see Figure 14.1) to a new Conference Facility at the Earth Centre, Doncaster (see Figure 14.2) has generated a strategy capable of producing a wide range of carbon-neutral buildings able to survive in both polluted inner city sites and high occupation densities in more suburban locations.

A carbon-neutral building produces no overall CO_2 emissions to the atmosphere when energy flows are analysed over a typical year. Fossil fuel use is offset by renewable energy harvested by the building envelope – often using the national grid as a storage device enabling excess electrical

Figure 14.1
The New Parliamentary Building
(Architect: Michael Hopkins and Partners)

Figure 14.2
Aerial view of the new Conference
Building at the Earth Centre, Doncaster
(Architect: Bill Dunster Architects)

power to be exported to other sites. It is important that design teams try to achieve an overall carbon-neutral brief for each new project – as the UK building fabric is replaced at around 1.5% per annum, it is technically possible to achieve near carbon-neutral UK cities by the end of the next century using existing technology.

This work suggested that it is important to integrate a number of different renewable energy harvesting techniques, carefully reconciling the often conflicting parameters of daylight, passive solar gain, heat loss through the building skin, ventilation, and of course contact with the outside world. Photovoltaics are an important new technology enabling clean solar electricity to be generated in urban areas, but their use can only be justified if it is fully integrated with all the other climate modifying devices that are all competing for the same rays of sunlight. This study shows how some of these devices have been incorporated in buildings I have worked on, and tries to define the key design tools available to an architect wishing to realise a zero emissions urban workplace.

14.2 Identifying problems with existing approaches to low-energy buildings

The traditional approach to low-energy design has been to filter the adverse effects of the outside environment as heavily as possible, insulate the occupied space, limit the size of window openings, provide a gridwork of solar control blinds in front of those windows that remain, add layers of conservatory structures to south-facing facades with perhaps a few solar collectors or photovoltaic cells added on as bolt-on extras. This has often had a depressing effect on the interior, as the quest to neutralise the effects of the external environment on internal temperatures also deprived the occupants of contact with the world outside. This type of building often resulted in architecture that was obsessed with building physics, but provided very little contact with the outside world. I will attempt to show how attempting a holistic integration of these often conflicting design parameters has informed the detail design of several projects I have been closely involved with:

1. New Offices for MPs in Westminster – The New Parliamentary Building. Architects: Michael Hopkins and Partners. Currently nearing completion

Figure 14.3
The New Parliamentary Building
(Architect: Michael Hopkins and Partners)

2. New University Campus for Nottingham University. Architects: Michael Hopkins and Partners. Completed and shortly to be monitored (see Figure 14.4)

Figure 14.4
New University Campus
(Architect: Michael Hopkins and Partners)

3. Beddington Zero Emissions Development – London Borough of Sutton. Architects: Bill Dunster Architects (see Figure 14.5).

Figure 14.5
Beddington Zero Emissions
Development

14.3 Making renewable energy viable by minimising demand

The challenge appeared to be how to integrate as many functions as possible into a single element of construction, at the same time as optimising its overall performance. Adding more technical parameters into the design of each individual component makes the design more difficult, but the duplication of function can enable passive environmental features to be incorporated without additional cost. The primary objective for us is to design the building fabric as the primary or "passive" internal climate modifier, and only then introduce "active" building engineering systems to assist the building fabric to recycle ambient energy. The effective application of passive devices reduces the requirements for high-grade thermal and electrical energy to the level where they can be economically supplied from renewable sources. It becomes important to fully integrate solar technologies with those essential elements of the building fabric that must be provided to achieve shelter. As each passive system becomes optimised, and active renewable energy harvesting components such as photovoltaic cells become more affordable and building integrated, near zero energy input buildings become increasingly feasible. Any building can become carbon neutral if finances are unlimited and enough PV is included in its external envelope – however, a more viable design strategy must seek to minimise the demand for energy in order to minimise the area of PVs needed to match it. Incorporating PVs is often relatively straightforward, whereas minimising the building's energy loads so that the photovoltaics make a meaningful contribution to its overall energy requirements is often more difficult.

14.4 Combining thermal storage with ventilation: air-cooled structures

In a conventional speculative office building in central London a structural floor plate would be invisible, hidden by suspended ceilings and raised floors. An energy-conscious building will try to maximise visible areas of exposed thermal mass, providing large low temperature radiant surfaces that behave as a thermal flywheel. Rooms need to be higher to allow air to stratify below the ceiling under its own buoyancy, at the same time as scooping as much daylight as possible from the window wall – suggesting a thin-walled sinusoidal section concrete slab, that both expresses the air supply to the room at the same time as using the minimum resources to provide a clear span of nearly 14m. The need to expose thermal mass suggests that the floor could be fairfaced reinforced concrete – omitting the suspended ceiling, with the concrete mix constituents designed to maximise daylight reflection. To satisfy the New Parliamentary Building (see Figure 14.6) brief requirement for an occupied room temperature range of 22°C + or − 2°C with the use of passive cooling required an in-depth understanding of heat flowing into and out of a typical MP's room. As the facade has an overall high level of thermal resistance, most of the room daytime heat gain is retained, so that for the majority of the year there is a heat excess to be managed.

The heat is stored in the structural floor slabs (see Figure 14.7) to deal with the night heat loss, and to avoid boost heating prior to morning occupancy. Night ventilation in summer is used to remove any daytime surplus from the building. High thermal capacity room surfaces with a density range up to 200kg/m² of floor area are used as the heat storage medium because of their ability to function with small changes in temperature difference and to take full advantage of both radiative and convective heat transfer. A simple structural floor has become a radiator, a daylight reflector, a ceiling finish, a ventilation air duct and a thermal store. It costs more than its monofunctional predecessor, but less than the sum of all of the above features if they were made as individual components. It is also far more durable, and, if carefully designed, will have a lower embodied energy content and fare far better in a life-cycle costing analysis.

Figure 14.6
Sectional model of the New Parliamentary Building

14.5 Solar-powered groundwater heating and cooling

This extensive thermal storage has enabled a lower grade source of winter heating and summer cooling to be used: in the form of groundwater extracted from 60m below the building providing a constant source of

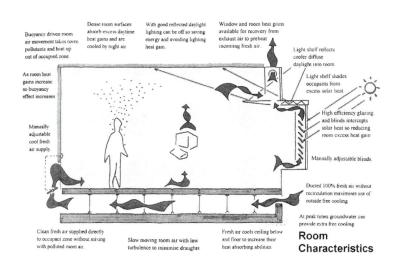

Figure 14.8
Energy supply and demand

Figure 14.7
Precast white concrete slab stacked ready for assembly on site

water at around 13°C. In winter modest boilers are required to heat the ventilation air, and in summer the groundwater becomes a useful source of cooling (see Figure 14.8). Further research has indicated that in cooling mode there would be an excellent match between peak summer photovoltaic output and peak summer groundwater pumping loads. The additional cost of the photovoltaic installation could be offset by the omission of an active cooling system.

14.6 Using breathing facades to power the ventilation system

In a similar way, the solar shading in the external wall can become a solar hot air collector if dark venetian blinds are installed within a ventilated cavity – allowing only $25W/m^2$ summer solar gain in a 3.6m south frontage room around 4m deep. Figure 14.9 shows the air temperatures created within a ventilated window cavity and indicates the potential of making a window into a solar hot air collector (at the same time this reduces heat transfer into the room). Within a few years we expect to see amorphous silicon-coated photovoltaic venetian blind blades that will be capable of generating modest amounts of electricity to run small permanent magnet fans that could keep the cavities ventilated at peak thermal loads and, at the same time, functioning as a useful solar hot air collector in the heating season (see Figure 14.10). Solar gains can be removed before the incident energy has entered the building by linking the facade into the building's extract ventilation system, and either dumped in summer or recovered through heat exchangers at roof level. By taking incoming fresh air into the building at roof level, not only is heat and coolth recovery made possible, but ground-level air pollution from traffic is significantly reduced – a key criterion in most city centres. In the New Parliamentary Building, this "building lung" is accommodated in a rooftop turret incorporating a 3.6m diameter moisture-recovering thermal wheel achieving 86% efficient heat recovery providing 100% fresh air to the rooms inside. This technology

Figure 14.9
CFD simulation of air temperatures within a ventilated air cavity

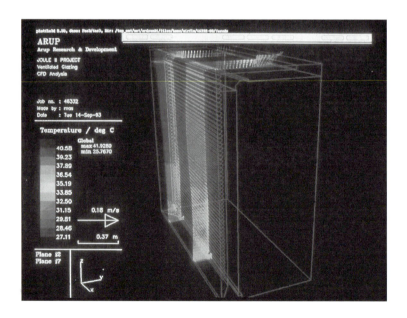

enabled the design team to avoid the health problems of recirculated stale air, without an excessive energy penalty. Providing this type of mechanically driven heat recovery uses very low powered fans it can be more energy-efficient than a naturally ventilated building.

14.7   Taking stock and minimising fan power

An examination of the overall system energy consumption showed that using a combination of the technologies discussed above would result in an annual energy consumption of around 65kWh/m²/y. Figure 14.11 shows available energy from wind and solar power.

Not all these features have been incorporated into the New Parliamentary Building as built – Ove Arup predict an overall energy consumption of around 96kWh/m²/y. The next step in our research program examined ways of reducing the reliance on electrically driven fans, investigating the potential for thermal buoyancy, wind-driven ventilation and photovoltaics.

A research test rig funded by the EU at the Conphoebus solar research station in Sicily began by using mechanical ventilation fans to bring roof-level fresh air down vertical ducts built into the facade to supply each floor. However, a test installation with larger thermal flues built onto the existing Conphoebus low-energy office building (see Figure 14.12) achieved an exhaust airspeed of 1.5 metres per second exit velocity and satisfactory internal comfort conditions by taking fresh air on the north facade at each floor level, and using passive stack ventilation with no fans.

14.8   Heat recovery from photovoltaics used to drive a ventilation chimney

Translucent insulation achieving around 0.7W/m²/°C was applied to the exhaust air shafts to increase the performance of the vertical ducts as solar hot air collectors, effectively increasing airflow through the rooms. A later test rig substituted a skin of monocrystalline photovoltaic cells in place of the translucent insulation – and the electricity output was monitored at the same time as recording the heat recovered within the ventilated cavity at different air flow rates. We concluded that in the UK the winter heat loss through a glazed duct of this configuration outweighed the considerable benefits of passive solar gain, illustrating the importance of not integrating large areas of building-integrated photovoltaics in the UK climate without checking the heat lost through the glazed wall. However, this configuration could be useful when combined with amorphous silicon (whose output is less affected by temperature) and applied in warmer Mediterranean climates.

14.9   Daylight reflection systems

The windows incorporate light shelves to maintain daylight levels at the rear of rooms when the solar shading is in use, avoiding the blinds down lights on scenario with its consequent luminaire heat gain and energy penalty. The light shelf has been incorporated into a sealed unit with an internal corrugated reflector designed to maximise high altitude reflections, and to reject lower altitude direct solar gain. A partly internal, partly external light shelf shades the area close to the window on southern elevations and redistributes daylight deeper into the floor plate, doubling daylight levels on the working plane at 4m from the facade on highly shaded north facades. The design challenge must be to integrate photovoltaics at the same time as achieving excellent daylight levels deep inside the rooms.

Figure 14.10
Photovoltaic blinds in a ventilated cavity

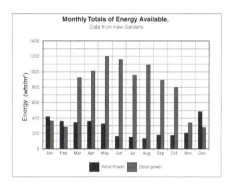

Figure 14.11
Energy available from first Joule study

Figure 14.12
Conphoebus low-energy office building with two-storey test facade

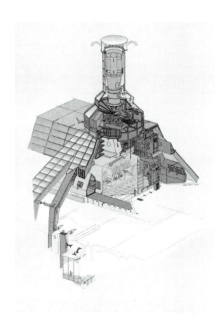

Figure 14.13
Ventilation diagram for the New
Parliament Building

14.10 The artificial lighting system

By mounting compact fluorescent light fittings within the internal light shelf, and fitting daylight sensors with variable dimming, it was possible to switch the artificial lights on only as daylight levels began to fall. The artificial light is reflected off the ceiling and arrives on the working plane at similar paths to the daylight, allowing seamless integration between both light sources, and minimising energy consumed by lighting. Using this strategy it is possible to reduce the annual lighting energy consumption from 44kWh/m²/y on a good practice contemporary office in the UK to 19kWh/m²/y on our research model.

14.11 The mechanical ventilation strategy

The Parliamentary Building incorporates low pressure drop air handling, heat recovery and duct components (see Figure 14.13) – specified to achieve a ventilation power target of 1W/l/s of air supplied. The fan total pressure generated by supply and extract fans together is 640Pa, with fan efficiencies of 65%. Typically the air handling plant component face velocities are 1.2m/s with the filters at 0.8m/s. The environmental strategy allows the same full fresh air system to serve all room types, allowing future changes of room function without requiring a services refit. Not only does this make the services compatible with the longer life needed on public buildings, but it considerably reduces the embodied energy content of the engineering services during the building lifetime.

Nottingham University New Campus has further refined the ultra low pressure drop air distribution (see below).

Figure 14.14 shows the University of Nottingham air-handling unit schematic

Both projects incorporate rotating hygroscopic thermal heat recovery wheels; however, the Nottingham Campus incorporates an evaporative humidifier to cool down extract air in summer before it passes through the heat recovery system, thus allowing coolth to be transferred to the supply airstream without air recirculation, providing up to 6°C free cooling at peak summer loads. Adding both supply air heating and cooling loads on a good practice modern office building will require 109kWh/m²/y. This can be reduced to 18kWh/m²/y using the low pressure drop heat recovery ventilation system in combination with an air-cooled thermally massive structural system.

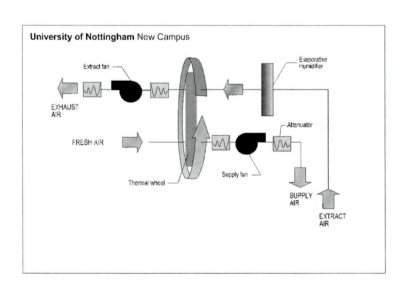

Figure 14.14
University of Nottingham air-handling
unit concept

Figure 14.15 shows a conceptual urban low-energy office with wind driven ventilation and low pressure drop internal air distribution.

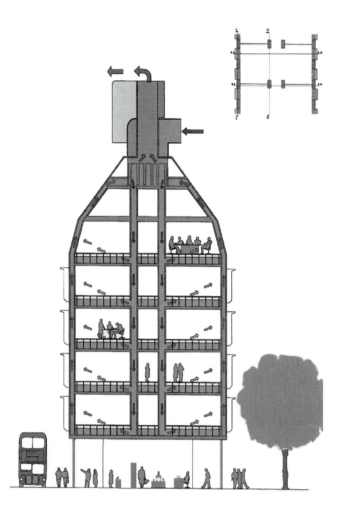

Figure 14.15
Section through low-energy urban office
(Joule 2 Research Programme)

14.12 Adding wind-driven ventilation to reduce fan use

Nottingham University New Campus uses corridors as ultra low pressure drop return air paths with stair towers as vertical chimneys. By placing the heat recovery air-handling units above the stair towers, it is possible to bypass the mechanical ventilation system and allow natural ventilation of

Figure 14.16
Nottingham University wind cowls with photovoltaic atrium roofs in foreground

Figure 14.17
View of the Beddington ZED project
from the London Road

these communal spaces in mid-season, when heating and cooling loads are lowest. Each room has tilt/turn opening windows, allowing most rooms to be naturally ventilated and effectively allowing a mixed-mode ventilation option. Rotating wind-driven cowls track away from the prevailing wind down to wind speeds of 2m/s, ensuring flow reversal never happens and that a constant negative pressure is maintained at the head of each stairwell.

Further research work has been undertaken in conjunction with the CSTB in Nantes, where rotating wind-driven cowls combining both extract and supply air have been developed. Current work at Beddington Zero Emissions Development – a solar urban village for the Peabody Trust in the London Borough of Sutton – indicates that ultra low pressure drop heat recovery can be combined with fan free wind-driven ventilation systems.

Figure 14.17 shows a view of the Beddington ZED project.

14.13 Integrating photovoltaic panels

Providing that ultra low pressure drop air distribution is specified and combined with most of the building components described earlier, it is possible to reduce the annual electrical load to the point where it can be met by grid-connected building integrated photovoltaics. The study undertaken by Conphoebus showed that photovoltaics could be integrated with return air flues built into the ventilated facade system; however, this would be more appropriate for passive cooling applications in Mediterranean climates, as the heat loss from glass ducts in winter reduced the efficiency of the heat recovery system in more temperate applications.

However, the annual energy performance of a theoretical urban model loosely based on the Parliamentary Building geometry was simulated using real time UK climatic data, and proved that in the UK winter wind power and summer photo-electric generation complemented each other excellently. This enabled the fan run times to be reduced to the point where the total energy consumption became $27kWh/m^2$ floor area/y. If additional areas of high-efficiency photovoltaic cells were incorporated on the sloping roof surfaces, taken over a year's duration, this design could produce as much energy as it consumed. As PV prices drop and efficiencies rise, it will be increasingly viable to build low rise zero energy urban offices.

Table 14.1 gives a comparison between the University of Nottingham buildings and a typical good practice building.

Table 14.1
Comparative data (1)

		Base model of good practice	University of Nottingham faculty buildings
		kWh/m²/y	kWh/m²/y
Gas	Heating & hot water	100.0	66.0
Electricity	Refrigeration	17.0	2.5
	Fans & pumps	39.0	2.0
	Lights	35.1	13.1
Total	Gas & electricity	191.1	83.6
CO_2	kg/m²	96.0	27.0
Annual CO_2 reduction		2556 tonnes	

The area of photovoltaic cells integrated into the atrium roofs on Nottingham University New Campus annually generates 60,000kWh and provides enough electrical energy to power the air-handling units and heat-recovery systems – enabling a lower annual energy consumption than a naturally ventilated building, within a construction budget of £900/m² of floor area including the EU Thermie contribution.

The Nottingham University mechanical ventilation system only required an annual average of 0.37 Watts per l per s of air supplied. This resulted in a total fan electrical consumption of 7871kWh/y/air-handling unit. A total of six low velocity air-handling units mounted on three different sized faculty buildings required a total fan electrical consumption of 51,000kWh/y, which could be produced by 256 1497 × 1170mm size PV modules integrated into the middle third of each atrium roof (to minimise loss of daylight to atrium-facing rooms) each containing 88 BP monocrystalline-toughened inner, low-iron outer glass cells. Four three-phase inverters were used with each string of modules connecting to specially extruded glazing bars with PV wiring channels integrated. All modules face within 20° of south and are mounted at around 15° from the horizontal.

The modules are grid connected into the site-wide electrical distribution system, and have not been sized to meet the peak electrical loads of the air-handling units. On balance over a year they provide enough electrical energy to match the ventilation requirements. The base electrical load of the university campus is always higher than the maximum PV output, making it unlikely that any renewable electricity is ever exported off site.

14.14 Nottingham University PV specification

The PV installation (see Figures 14.18 and 14.19) consists of 450m² of BP Solar monocrystalline 125 × 125mm pseudo square cells mounted in single glazing, giving a peak total output of 54.3kW.

The single glazing consists of two panes of 6mm heat soaked toughened glass with the upper pane of low-iron glass. Each glazed module is supplied with pre-wired cables and plug-in connections.

Figure 14.19
Details of the PV mounted on the atrium
roof at the University of Nottingham

Each nominal 1200 × 1500mm module of 88 cells has:

Rated output   = 212.1W
Open circuit voltage U_o = 53.5V
MPP voltage U_{max} = 44V
Short circuit current I_x = 5.2A
MPP current I_{max} = 4.8A

There are either 8 or 11 strings of modules in each atrium connected to
either a 12 or 18.5kW inverter/power conditioning unit (PCU). These feed
into the main three-phase power distribution busbars in each building.

14.15 The next step: taking fans out of the ventilation system?

A new conference building at the Earth Centre, built to tight budgets, tries to
co-ordinate a variety of renewable energy features to maximise the thermal
and solar benefit of each season. This building uses a small number of roof-

mounted polycrystalline photovoltaic cells to power pumps connecting roof-mounted solar hot water collectors to an underground highly insulated hot water store. The electrical output from the photovoltaics occurs at exactly the same time as the effective output from the solar hot water panels. The following key design decisions helped generate the near carbon-neutral building shown in Figure 14.20:

1. A sense of arrival at the hub of the Earth Centre has buried the conference centre into the hillside. Earth sheltered buildings stay cooler in summer, are less affected by wind, and lose less heat in winter. The roofs of the new rooms will be coloured sedum, forming a mound of colour on the sloping grass hillside.
2. The difficult ground conditions caused by the coal shale means the building has to float like a raft in a sea of shingle.
3. The foundations have been formed into an insulated concrete tank, which when filled with water heated by solar thermal panels enables the building to store warmth from the summer to heat the building in winter.
4. The main conference hall sits above the water tank on a carpet of insulation with its ceiling inclined towards south to provide a mounting position for the solar hot water panels. These panels then provide a waterproof roof.
5. A circular ramp climbs steadily around the central auditorium giving disabled access to a number of perimeter smaller conference chambers and allowing all visitors to climb to the viewing point on the Planet Earth Gallery roof.
6. All rooms are top lit with south light. In winter the sunlight provides daylight and warmth, reducing the need to switch on electric lights in daytime without losing heat from large areas of glass at night. Overhanging eaves help reduce excessive heat gain in summer.
7. The conference centre is super insulated with 300mm of insulation on all walls, roof and floor. Super insulated buildings lose so little heat through their enclosing surfaces that most energy is lost through the ventilation system. It is important to maintain good fresh air in a conference room – otherwise visitors become drowsy. Mechanical ventilation systems with fans are thermally efficient but tend to use relatively large amounts of high grade electrical energy, whilst naturally ventilated chambers have high heating requirements to ensure that the large volumes of incoming fresh air are heated adequately to avoid discomfort.
8. The new conference centre uses heat recovery to minimise the winter heat loss. Outgoing stale air preheats incoming fresh air without the contamination or recirculation that can cause sick-building syndrome. By oversizing the heat recovery units, and minimising the pressure drop through the ventilation system, it is possible to channel wind into the rooms using positive-pressure wind catchers at the

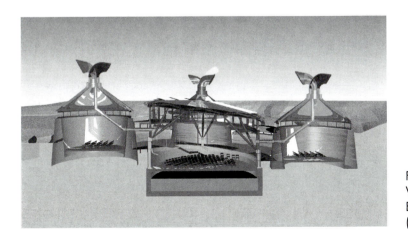

Figure 14.20
View of the Conference Building at the Earth Centre, Doncaster
(Architect: Bill Dunster Architects)

same time as exhausting the stale air using wind suction. This enables the ventilation system to work without fans whilst maintaining similar air quality. Special rotating cowls have been developed in wind tunnels that will turn to catch the slightest wind, merging some of the same ideas found in a Kentish oast house with an Iranian *bad-gir* wind tower.

9. The hillside is restrained by local stone rubble used to fill galvanised wire gabion cages. This avoids using energy intensive reinforced concrete, and allows the materials to be easily reclaimed at the end of the building's life. The massive rock surfaces keep the rooms cool in summer and store heat from sunny to dull days in winter.

10. Wherever possible reclaimed materials salvaged from the Doncaster area have been resourced, thus recycling unwanted urban infrastructure to create a useful new building. Reclaimed joists are resawn to create floorboards and ceilings, and a lamella (grid shell roof) in the entrance foyer uses this reclaimed timber to create an advanced long span structure. Energy intensive metals such as aluminium are used sparingly, often where strength and a low weight are important in the rotating wind cowls – or for glazing bars and roof surfaces where longevity and low maintenance are important. All steel sections are reclaimed directly from local demolition sites and fabricated into new components on site.

11. Back-up heating towards the end of the winter, or on particularly cold days, is provided by a large woodburning stove with a back boiler feeding hot water to a chain of salvaged cast iron radiators in each room. Trees absorb CO_2 from the atmosphere as they grow, giving the same amount out again when burnt as firewood. This allows any extra heating required to be from renewable energy sources, and is more or less carbon neutral, with the heating system generating no net CO_2 emissions to the atmosphere, providing that the wood fuel is sourced from local sustainably managed forests.

12. A small vertical axis wind generator is mounted on the boiler flue, providing some electricity to run lighting. The high electrical loads needed to run the conference IT system and high-powered audio visual system will be provided by the Earth Centre's mains electrical grid, with a large proportion supplied by the new PV canopy designed by Feilden Clegg Bradley (see Chapter 11).

14.16 The need for a site overview of energy use

It is pointless to build PV-powered buildings that cannot be reached by electric public transportation systems, as fossil fuel use and pollution by cars can far exceed that used by the workplace enclosure. (It is also important to check that the energy invested in the total installation and manufacture, including the support structure, is paid back by energy generated by the PV system within a reasonable pay-back period.)

14.17 Conclusion

It is clear that any building can become carbon neutral if enough PVs are included, or green electricity is purchased from some remote windfarm. This is short-term thinking and can easily be dismissed by deeper engineering analysis – as buildings become increasingly capable of generating their own power, it will become important to measure all incoming and outgoing energy flows in $kWh/m^2/y$. The demand for green electricity has already outstripped supply, making it important to include renewable energy harvesting devices on as many new buildings as possible. Photovoltaics are an expensive technology, but providing they are integrated into a thermally efficient building with low-energy requirements in the first place they will make carbon-neutral urban fabric possible.

REFERENCE

1.   Data from Ove Arup & Partners.

ACKNOWLEDGEMENTS

The following research studies and project teams have informed this chapter.

The Energy Efficient Workplace
Joule 2 Contract No JOU2-CT92-0235
Engineering research and prototype development for low-energy buildings
Participants:
Architects and project co-ordinator: Michael Hopkins and Partners – Bill Dunster, consultant
Ove Arup and Partners – environmental engineers
Bartenbach Lichtlabor – lighting engineer
MBM Metalbau Mockmuhl Gmbh – prototype development
Technical Blinds – solar control prototype development
Conphoebus Scri – testing

Renewable Energy Sources for the Workplace
Joule 2 Contract No JOU2-CT93-0351
Office and Public Buildings incorporating Wind/Solar Buoyancy/Photovoltaic Powered Ventilation Systems
Participants:
Michael Hopkins and Partners – architects and project co-ordinator – Bill Dunster, consultant
Ove Arup and Partners – environmental engineers
Centre Scientifique et Technique du Batiment – aerodynamic engineers
Conphoebus Scri – photovoltaic research

Nottingham University New Campus – Faculty Buildings
Thermie Contract No BU-169-97-GB
Participants:
Nottingham University
Michael Hopkins and Partners – architects with consulting by Bill Dunster
Ove Arup and Partners – structural and environmental engineers
Gardiner and Theobald – cost consultants
Battle McCarthy – ecological masterplanners
Mace – project management
ABB Airtech AB

BEDZED – Zero Emissions Development for the Peabody Trust
Partners :
Bill Dunster architects – architects
Ove Arup and Partners – environmental engineers
Gardiner and Theobald – cost consultants
Ellis and Moore – structural engineers
BioRegional Development Group – community liaison/environmental consultants
Kingston University – Green Audit – prototype testing and environmental research

The Earth Centre – Phase 2 – new Conference Centre
Partners:
Contractors and client – Taylor Woodrow
Bill Dunster architects – architects
Ove Arup and Partners – environmental engineers
Gleeds – cost consultants
Mark Lovell Design – structural engineers

15

Conclusion

Randall Thomas

Good PV architecture might be considered to be more difficult than good architecture because there is an additional factor to integrate into the design. Nonetheless, the preceding studies have shown that PVs can readily be adopted to, or even form, a starting point for high-quality, stimulating, creative, diversified, environmentally friendly architecture.

A rapid survey of PVs indicates a number of key areas of progress:

- Community level integration.
- Integrated building solutions.
- Development.
- Government support.

Communities

There is an encouraging growing realisation that the optimum use of photovoltaics needs to be seen in a planning context.

Density of occupation, street widths, park areas, and massing of buildings are all interrelated with maximising the solar potential of an area, of which PVs are a key element. Architects and planners have an especially important role to play here.

Buildings

It is becoming clear to more designers that PVs must be considered as part of the overall environmental design of the building. For example, reduction of the electrical energy demand through greater use of daylighting will increase the percentage of the demand that can be supplied by PVs.

Considerable effort is also going into incorporating PVs into traditional building products such as roof tiles or glazing systems. This is encouraging because the less special PVs become, the lower their cost will be.

Work is also underway on storage systems which would allow better use of "waste" heat from PVs.

In the near future we can expect to see designers turn their attention to integrating PVs into the refurbishment of buildings and, particularly, their roof scapes.

Development

Research and development is significant. A photovoltaic cell with a 32% efficiency has been developed using a 3-junction technology of gallium indium phosphorous/gallium arsenide/germanium(1). Commercially available thin film module efficiencies varying from 8.3% to 12.1% and higher are regularly reported in the specialist press(2).

Production capacity is increasing. A factory in Ohio is being built to provide 100MW annually of thin film cadmium telluride cells. Another just opened in Germany to produce 10–12MW of polycrystalline cells. The company responsible for the plant expects the cost of PV power to be halved by 2010(3). To put these figures into perspective the world currently needs 10,000GW of power(4). So we have a way to go. One report estimates that factories with annual output of 500MWp would lower PV prices to levels competitive with conventional power due to high levels of automation and economies of scale(5).

Government support

Government support varies with the country, but is on the increase. In Germany, for example, proposed new legislation guarantees that producers of PV electricity will receive a significant subsidy – six times more than the current level; support will reduce in time as PVs become more competitive(6).

The intention, of course, is for the government to help break out of what has been called the solar supply and demand Catch 22(7): prices are high because demand is low, demand is low because prices are high.

In the UK a number of initiatives are underway, including encouragement of PVs in schools and ongoing support for demonstration projects.

Summary

The seedlings of a photovoltaic architecture are developing in the UK. Growth would be faster if costs were lower, if product information were more readily available, if architects and clients had easy access to tried and tested designs and demonstration projects, if connection to the national grid were easier – the list could be continued. The wheel is turning – the future lies in increasing its speed.

Figure 15.1
The world's first solar-powered Ferris wheel in Santa Monica, California(8)

REFERENCES

1. Anon, (1999), News. Renewable Energy World 2(6), p. 17.
2. Anon, (2000), News. Renewable Energy World, 3(1), p. 14.
3. Anon, (2000), Achievements and Potential. Renewable Energy World, 3(1), p. 94.
4. Gratzel, M. (2000), Powering the planet. Nature, 403(676), p. 363.
5. Anon, (1999), PV – Breaking the Solar Impasse, Renewable Energy World, 2(6), p. 95.
6. See reference 2, p. 8.
7. See reference 5, p. 96.
8. Anon, (1998), News. Electrical Review, 231(22), p. 3.

Appendix A

A.1   The Photovoltaic Effect

This is the basic process by which a PV cell converts solar radiation into electricity. In crystalline silicon cells a p–n junction ("p" for positive, "n" for negative) is formed (Figure 2.1) by diffusing phosphorous into the silicon and introducing a small quantity of boron. This results in an electric field being formed. When photons, "particles" of solar energy, are absorbed by a PV cell, electrons under the influence of the field move out towards the surface. This flow or current is "harnessed" by an external circuit with a load.

A typical monocrystalline cell of, say, 100mm by 100mm in bright sunshine of 1000W/m² might produce a current of 3 amps at 0.5 volts giving 1.5 watts of power.

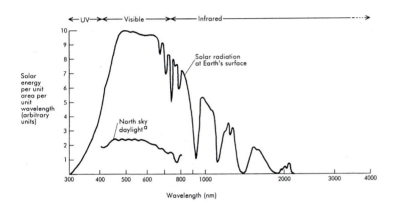

Figure A.1
Spectral distribution of solar radiation at the earth's surface

Figure A.2
Spectral response of a monocrystallline PV cell

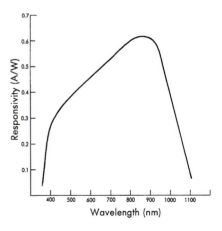

A.2   The Environment and PVs

Figure A.1 shows the spectral distribution, ie the amount of radiation at various wavelengths, of solar radiation.

Solar radiation can be divided into direct and diffuse radiation. In the UK the diffuse component is high – in London 60% of the total annual irradiation on a horizontal surface is diffuse and in Glasgow the figure is very similar at 61%. The radiation climate is also very variable and can quickly change from bright sunshine to heavy clouds. Ideally, the total PV installation from array to inverter will react optimally to all the characteristics of the environment.

PV cells respond mainly to visible radiation (wavelengths of approximately 400nm–700nm) but also to some UV (below 400nm) and some infrared (above 700nm). Figure A.2 shows the response of a monocrystalline cell; amorphous silicon cells have a somewhat different curve with a peak between 500nm–600nm. (The absorption characteristics of PV cells obviously affect the design. For example, normal glass contains traces of iron which cause the glass to absorb strongly in the visible green range. Since PV cells can use this energy, PV modules incorporate low-iron glass.)

Fortunately, PVs respond to diffuse radiation as well as direct radiation. Output varies with intensity as shown in Figure A.3. A heavily overcast sky might have an intensity of 50W/m² with a diffuse component of 95–100% and a cloudless blue sky might have an intensity of 900W/m² with a diffuse component of 20%.

Efficiency also varies somewhat with intensity with slightly lower values at lower intensities (1).

Figure A.3
Variation of module power with irradiance

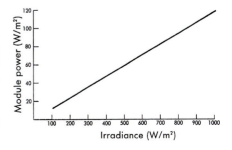

Figure A.4
Series and parallel arrangements

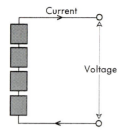

a. Four cells in series (higher voltage results)

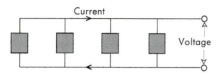

b. Four cells in parallel (higher current results)

Figure A.5
Current/voltage (I-V) curve

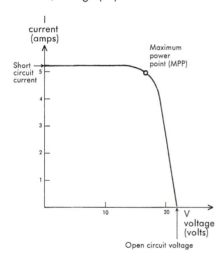

Figure A.6
Typical I-V curves at varying irradiances

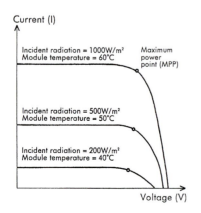

A.3 How to read a PV module data sheet

Firstly, read with caution as there is not yet a uniform way of presenting information. In addition to the construction and physical characteristics and warranty conditions, the following items are likely to be included:

1. Cell type, eg monocrystalline silicon.

2. Cell specifications, eg 36 series-connected cells. (See Figure A.4 for series and parallel arrangements.)

3. Physical Conditions
   There may be an indication of the wide-ranging conditions in which PV modules can be used. For example:
   Temperature: −40°C to 85°C
   Relative humidity: 0% to 100%
   Wind loading: Up to 80km/h

4. Electrical characteristics (eg for a module of 1.2m × 0.5m)
   Nominal peak power   90.0W
   Voltage at peak power 18.5V
   Current at peak power 4.9A
   Short circuit current   5.2A

Figure A.5 shows a typical curve of module performance under STCs.

The short circuit current is the current at zero voltage. The corresponding point of zero current, ie "no connected loads", is the open circuit voltage. Power is the product of current and voltage and from the curve it can be determined that the maximum power of 90W is produced at a voltage of approximately 18.5V and a current of 4.9A.

At lower irradiances, power falls as shown in Figure A.6.

Note that the effect of varying temperature is also included. At higher temperatures efficiency falls (see Figure A.7(and more so with crystalline silicon cells than amorphous silicon. The effect of temperature on modules which include amorphous silicon can be complex, with a phenomenon of improved performance due to self-annealing compensating for an otherwise reduced efficiency(2). Manufacturers are currently studying this, in part because of its importance for building design. If performance does not drop off significantly with higher temperatures the need to ventilate may disappear, thus increasing the designer's freedom. The PV module data sheet should give information about the variation of efficiency with temperature.

The function of a maximum power point tracker (Chapter 5) is to alter the effective load resistance so that the array will operate near the maximum power point in variable input conditions, ie under changing skies with their varying irradiances and in varying temperatures.

A.4 Shading

The effect of shading can be understood by referring to the series arrangement in Figure A.4. Because the cells are in series, if the performance of one cell is impaired by shading, the output current from the whole string is affected and minor shading can result in a major loss of energy. This is illustrated by Figure A.8.

A.5 Mismatch

Mismatch refers to the losses due to differences in the I–V characteristics (Figure A.5) of the modules in a PV array.

In Chapter 2 mismatch losses have been included in the correction factor, K.

A.6 Balance of system losses

In Chapter 2 the balance of system (BOS) loss, L, was mentioned. It accounts for factors such as the following, which are listed with very approximate values (expressed as a percentage of the array output ("E") in Chapter 2):

- Cable losses – 1–3%
- Losses at the PCU and particularly at the inverter – say 10–15%
- Metering and utility interface control losses – less than 1%

Thus, an overall figure of 0.8 for L is a reasonable starting point.

A.7 Performance ratio and sizing

The following discussion continues the procedure started in Chapter 2.

The Performance Ratio (PR) is the final yield (kWh/kWp/day) divided by the reference yield. It can be expressed either as a decimal fraction or as a percentage.

The reference yield is based on the in-plane irradiance and represents the theoretically available energy per day per kWp installed. Typical PR values are 60–75% but higher values are achieved.

Rough array sizing is sometimes done using estimates of the PR in the following way:

1. Assume a value for the PR, say, 0.7.
2. Determine the solar irradiation on the actual array. For example, in our Chapter 2 example we have $920kWh/m^2/y \times 0.15$ (module efficiency) $\times 0.95$ correction factor for tilt and azimuth or $131kWh/m^2/y$.
3. The output of the PV system, then, will be: $0.7 \times 131kWh/m^2/y = 92kWh/m^2/y$.

The PR equals the product of K and L in Chapter 2.

A.8 Inverter selection

As mentioned in Chapter 5, inverter selection is a key element in the PV system design process.

Figure A.9(a) shows generalised inverter performance and A.9(b) the performance of one of the small inverters used at the BRE Environmental Building (Figure 5.2(b)).

With all inverters, efficiency is impaired at very low levels of irradiance and, since there are energy losses in the inverter, there is a point below which it does not make sense to use the PV DC electricity.

Figure A.7
Cell efficiency as a function of temperature

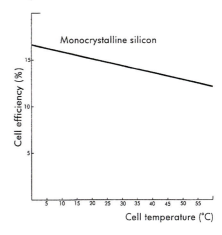

Figure A.8
The effect of shading

PV cells connected horizontally in series of four.

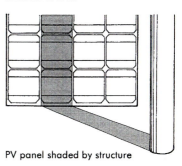

PV panel shaded by structure

The effect of shading one cell in series is analogous to a blocked hosepipe. The flow of water/current is limited by the blockage/performance of the shaded cell.

Figure A.9
Inverter performance

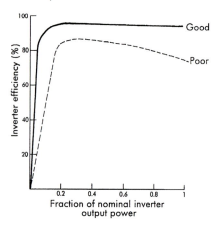

a) generalised inverter performance

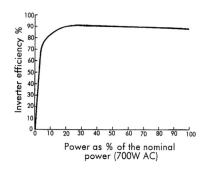

b) Characteristics of the inverters used at the BRE Environmental Building

Similarly, with all inverters, operating conditions in the UK mean that for a significant part of the time efficiency is in the 20–80% range. In practice, this means that a balance needs to be struck between losing some of the available energy at very high irradiance levels and operating at a somewhat higher efficiency in lower irradiation levels. Current experience in the UK indicates optimal performance is at a sizing of approximately 75–80% of the array rating(3). This is broadly in line with a European suggestion that optimal performance may be obtained using inverters with a rating of 70–90% of the nominal rating of the array(4); however, as the authors say, "this will depend on the climate and the shape of the inverter performance characteristic."

Again, each situation needs to be analysed and this is normally done at a later detailed design stage.

A.9   Earthing and lightning protection

Earthing and lightning protection is an area that requires an engineering assessment of the building's construction and electrical system and advice from an electrical engineer.

The design of PV modules isolates the electrical system from the supporting structure, eg the module frame. Broadly speaking, most UK PV systems do not connect the DC side of the electrical system to earth. The supporting structure, on the other hand, in most systems is earthed. The AC side of the system is connected to the building's normal electrical system's earth.

With regard to lightning protection, PV installations do not require lightning protection systems per se. Protection against deleterious effects to sensitive parts of the installation is often provided by surge protection devices. If the building has a lightning protection system, common practice is to connect the supporting structure to the lightning protection system.

REFERENCES

1.   Mason, N.B., Bruton, T.M. and Heasman, K.C, (1997), kWh/kWp Energy Production from LGBG Cell Modules in Northern Europe. Paper presented at the 12th German National PV Symposium Staffelstein.

2.   Noble, R., BP AMOCO, (2000), Private communication.

3.   Pearsall, N., Newcastle Photovoltaics Applications Centre, (1998), Private communication.

3.   Anon. (undated), Photovoltaic Technologies and their Future Potential. Commission of the European Communities, Directorate-General for Energy (XVII). EAB Energie – Anlagen, Berlin.

FURTHER READING

Laukamp, H. (1994), The Basic German Electric Safety Standard and its Application to PV Systems. 12th European Conference PVSEC, Amsterdam.

Halcrow Gilbert Associates, (1993), Grid Connection of Photovoltaic Systems. ETSU S 1394-P1. ETSU: Harwell.

References and Bibliography

We list below a number of sources of information (in most cases previously referred to in the text) that we have found particularly useful.

Publications

1. Newcastle Photovoltaics Applications Centre. Architecturally Integrated Grid-Connected PV Facade at the University of Northumbria. ETSU S/P2/00171/REP, ETSU: Harwell.

2. 21 AD Architectural Digest for the 21st Century Photovoltaics. Eds. Roaf, S. and Walker, V. Oxford Brookes University.

3. Sick, F. and Erge, T., Eds, (1996), Photovoltaics in Buildings. James and James, London.

4. Humm, O. and Togweiler, P., (1993), Photovoltaics in Architecture. Birkhauser, Basel.

5. ECOTEC, ECD and NPAC, (1998), The Value of Electricity Generated from Photovoltaic Power Systems in Buildings. ETSU S/P2/00279/REP, ETSU: Harwell.

6. BP Solar, (1993), A Study of the Feasibility of Photovoltaic Modules as a Commercial Building Cladding Component. ETSU S/P2/00131/REP, ETSU: Harwell.

7. Studio E Architects, (1995), Photovoltaics in Buildings – A Survey of Design Tools. ETSU S/P2/00289/REP, ETSU: Harwell.

8. Halcrow Gilbert Associates, (1993), Grid Connection of Photovoltaic Systems. ETSU S 1394-P1, ETSU: Harwell.

9. Laukamp, H., (1994), The Basic German Electric Safety Standard and its Application to PV Systems. 12th European Conference PVSEC, Amsterdam.

10. Studio E Architects, (2000), Photovoltaics in Buildings BIPV Projects. ETSU S/P2/00328/REP, ETSU: Harwell.

Web Sites

BP Solar Web site: www.bp.com/bpsolar/index.html

US Department of Environment Web site: www.eren.doe.gov/pv/

Photovoltaic Power Systems web site:
www.iea-pvps.org

Glossary

Air Mass Number	A measure of the path length of sunlight through the atmosphere; expressed in comparison with unit path length where the sun is directly overhead; used to define the intensity and spectral distribution of sunlight.
Air Mass 1.5 (AM1.5)	The air mass number when the direction of the sun is 48° from the overhead position.
Alternating Current (AC)	Electric current in which the direction of flow is reversed at frequent intervals. The conventional grid supply is AC with an alternating frequency of 50Hz.
Amorphous	The condition of a solid in which the atoms are not arranged in an orderly pattern; not crystalline.
Balance of System (BOS)	The parts of a PV system other than the PV array itself, eg support structures, wiring, power conditioning units, etc.
Blocking Diode *	A diode connected in series to a PV string; it protects its modules from a reverse power flow and thus against the risk of thermal destruction of solar cells.
Bypass Diode *	A diode fitted in parallel with each cell string of a module to prevent overheating (hot spot) of a cell due to localised shading.
Conversion Efficiency	The ratio of the electrical energy produced by a PV cell (or module) to the energy from sunlight incident on the cell (or module). This is usually quoted for standard test conditions (STCs).
Crystalline	The condition of a solid where the atoms are arranged in an ordered pattern.
Daylight Factor *	The illuminance received at a point indoors, from a sky of known or assumed luminance distribution, expressed as a percentage of the horizontal illuminance outdoors from an unobstructed hemisphere of the same sky.
Diffuse Radiation	Solar radiation scattered by the atmosphere.
Direct Current (DC)	Electric current which flows in one direction.
Direct Radiation	Solar radiation transmitted directly through the atmosphere.
Electron	Negatively charged atomic particle; an electric current is the movement of electrons through a material.

Global Irradiance	The total irradiance (sunlight intensity) falling on a surface; the sum of the direct and diffuse irradiance.
Grid	1. The patterned metal contact on the top of the PV cell. 2. Common name for the electrical distribution system.
Irradiance	The intensity of solar radiation on a surface (W/m^2).
Irradiation	The amount of solar energy received on a surface (kWh/m^2).
Kilowatt (kW)	Unit of power equal to 1000W.
Kilowatt-hour (kWh)	Unit of energy equal to 1000Wh.
Load	Any device or appliance (or set of devices or appliances) which is using electrical power.
Low-emissivity Glass *	Glass with a low-emissivity coating on one surface; this allows short wavelength energy from the sun to pass through but reflects long wavelength energy back in, eg from a room.
Megawatt (MW)	Unit of power equal to 1,000,000W.
Megawatt-hour (MWh)	Unit of energy equal to 1,000,000Wh.
Micron	Unit of thickness equal to 10^{-6}m.
Multi-junction Cells *	Two (or more) different cells with more than one p–n junction; such an arrangement allows a greater portion of the sun's spectrum to be converted to electricity.
Nominal Array Power	The power rating of an array in Wp, as measured under standard test conditions (STCs).
Pascal (Pa)*	Unit of pressure $(1N/m^2)$.
Performance Ratio	Ratio of the system yield to the incident solar irradiation in the array plane.
Photon	A quantity of light having a fixed energy dependent on the wavelength of the light.
Photovoltaic (PV) Cell	Semiconductor device that converts light to electricity using the photovoltaic effect.
P–N Junction	A junction formed between two semiconductors of different doping types; the usual configuration for a PV cell.
Standard Test Conditions (STCs)	Standard test conditions are defined as an irradiance of $1000W/m^2$ at normal incidence, a spectral distribution of that irradiance equivalent to AM1.5 and a cell temperature of 25°C.

System Yield	Useful energy supplied to the load by the PV system expressed as a function of the nominal array power (kWh/day per kWp).
Uniformity Ratio *	The ratio of the minimum illuminance to the average illuminance.
Watt (W)	Unit of power.
Watt-hour (Wh)	Unity of energy; one Wh is consumed when one W of power is used for a period of one hour.
Watt peak (Wp)	Power output of a PV module under standard test conditions (STCs).

Notes:

1.   This glossary is almost entirely the work of the National Photovoltaic Applications Centre. The present authors have made only minor alterations to certain terms or introduced a small number of others indicated by an asterix. The definition of blocking diodes comes from Photovoltaics in Buildings (see bibliography) whilst the definition of bypass diodes come from "Stand alone PV systems: Guarantee of Results", ETSU S/P2/00237/REP.

2.   "Light" is used in common speech and in the text in a number of overlapping ways; the same is true for "sunlight". Visible radiation (400–700nm) is commonly called light but "light" is also used to describe a broader range of the electromagnetic spectrum. Similarly, "sunlight" is also referred to as sunshine or solar radiation. "Sunlight" is normally broken down into three components: ultraviolet, visible light and infrared.

Illustration Acknowledgements

The author and publishers would like to thank the following individuals and organisations for permission to reproduce material. We have made every effort to contact and acknowledge copyright holders, but if any errors have been made we would be happy to correct them at a later printing.

A number of the original illustrations have been redrawn for uniformity of style.

Figures 2.14, 2.15 and 2.16 were produced by the authors using the Meteonorm 3.0 computer program. The idea for the form comes from the ECOFYS solar energy irradiation disk.

Figure 1.1   Courtesy of Feilden Clegg Bradley Architects.
Figure 1.2   Courtesy of Akeler Developments.
Figure 1.3   Courtesy of ETSU/Department of Trade and Industry.
Figure 1.4   Anon. (undated), Photovoltaic Technologies and their Future Potential. Commission of the European Communities Directorate-General XVII for Energy. EAB Energie – Anlagen, Berlin.

Figure 2.3   Courtesy of NASA.
Figure 2.4   Courtesy of Akeler Developments.
Figure 2.5   Courtesy Max Fordham and Partners.
Figure 2.9   Sick, F. and Erge, T., Eds, (1996), Photovoltaics in Buildings. James and James, London.
Figure 2.13   ETSU R82 Climate in the UK.
Figure 2.17   Based on data from IT Power, (1996), Development of Photovoltaic Cladding Systems. ETSU S/P2/00216/REP, p.84. ETSU: Harwell.

Figure 3.4(a)   21 AD Architectural Digest for the 21st Century, Photovoltaics. Eds. Roaf, S. and Walker, V. Oxford Brookes University. pp.10–11, German 2000 Project. Roaf, S.
Figure 3.4(b)   Humm, O. and Toggweiler, P., (1993), Photovoltaics in Architecture. Birkhauser Verlag, Basel.
Figure 3.5   BP Solar, (1993), A Study of the Feasibility of Photovoltaic Modules as a Commercial Building Cladding Component. ETSU S/P2/00131/REP, ETSU: Harwell.
Figure 3.7(a)   Courtesy of Nigel Francis Photography, Oxford. "The Roaf House, Oxford."
Figure 3.7(b)   Courtesy of Redland Roofing. "PV700 integrated into a concrete tiled roof in Germany."
Figure 3.7(c)   Courtesy of Ganz and Muller Architects. "Ecole Polytechnique Fédérale de Lausanne, Switzerland."
Figure 3.7(d)   Courtesy of ETSU/Department of Trade and Industry. "The BP Solar showcase."
Figure 3.7(e)   Courtesy Bear Associates. "National Environmental Education Centre, Netherlands."
Figure 3.7(f)   Courtesy Max Fordham and Partners. "Building 16, The Building Research Establishment."
Figure 3.7(g)   Photo by Schüco International KG. "Schüco International HQ."
Figure 3.7(h)   Courtesy of BP Solar. "The Northumberland Building, University of Northumbria."
Figure 3.7(i)   Courtesy Dennis Gilbert. "Doxford Solar Office."
Figure 3.7(j)   Courtesy of Tenum AG, Switzerland. "The Öko-Bürohaus, Liestal."
Figure 3.7(k)   Courtesy Colt International Limited. "Tessin Innkeepers Association."
Figure 3.8   Courtesy BP Solar.
Figure 3.9   BP Solar (1993). A Study of the Feasibility of Photovoltaic Modules as a Commercial Building Cladding Component. ETSU S/P2/00131/REP, ETSU: Harwell.

Figure 4.2   Based on data from Halcrow Gilbert Associates.

Figure 5.2(a)   Courtesy Max Fordham and Partners
Figure 5.2(b)   Courtesy Max Fordham and Partners
Figure 5.3(a)   Courtesy SMA Regelsysteme D-34266 Niestetal.
Figure 5.3(b)   Courtesy SMA Regelsysteme D-34266 Niestetal.

Figure 5.4(a)	Courtesy Max Fordham and Partners
Figure 5.4(b)	Courtesy Max Fordham and Partners
Figure 5.5(a)	Sick, F. and Erge, T., Eds, (1996), Photovoltaics in Buildings. James and James, London.
Figure 5.5(b)	Courtesy BP Solar.
Figure 5.6	Courtesy David Lloyd Jones, Studio E Architects.
Figure A.1	Moon, P., (1940), Proposed standard solar radiation curve for engineering use. Journal of the Franklin Institute, V230, p. 583 courtesy of the Franklin Institute, Philadelphia, PA.
Figure A.2	Courtesy of BP Solar.
Figure A.3	21 AD Architectural Digest for the 21st Century, Photovoltaics. Eds. Roaf, S. and Walker, V. Oxford Brookes University. p.17–18, PV Module and System Development in Building Integration. Scott, R. D. W.
Figure A.6	Sick, F. and Erge, T., Eds, (1996), Photovoltaics in Buildings. James and James, London.
Figure A.7	Humm, O. and Togweiler, P., (1993), Photovoltaics in Architecture. Birkhauser Verlag, Basel.
Figure A.8	Sick, F. and Erge, T., Eds, (1996), Photovoltaics in Buildings. James and James, London.
Figure A.9	Anon. (undated), Photovoltaic Technologies and their Future Potential. Commission of the European Communities Directorate-General XVII for Energy. EAB Energie – Anlagen, Berlin.

Index

Page numbers in *italic* refer to illustrations